A-LEVEL
STUDENT GUIDE

AQA

Physical Education

Factors affecting participation in physical activity and sport

Symond Burrows
Michaela Byrne
Sue Young

Hodder Education, an Hachette UK company, Blenheim Court, George Street, Banbury, Oxfordshire OX16 5BH

Orders

Bookpoint Ltd, 130 Park Drive, Milton Park, Abingdon, Oxfordshire OX14 4SB

tel: 01235 827827

fax: 01235 400401

e-mail: education@bookpoint.co.uk

Lines are open 9.00 a.m.–5.00 p.m., Monday to Saturday, with a 24-hour message answering service. You can also order through the Hodder Education website: www.hoddereducation.co.uk

ISBN 978-1-5104-5546-7

First printed 2019

Impression number 5 4 3 2 1

Year 2023 2022 2021 2020 2019

This Student Guide has been written specifically to support students preparing for the AQA A-level examinations. The content has been neither approved nor endorsed by AQA and remains the sole responsibility of the author.

Typeset by Integra Software Services Pvt. Ltd., Pondicherry, India

Printed in Dubai

Cover photograph: biker 3 – stock.adobe.com

Hachette UK's policy is to use papers that are natural, renewable and recyclable products and made from wood grown in well-managed forests and other controlled sources. The logging and manufacturing processes are expected to conform to the environmental regulations of the country of origin.

Contents

Content Guidance

Questions & Answers

■Getting the most from this book

Exam tips

Advice on key points in the text to help you learn and recall content, avoid pitfalls, and polish your exam technique in order to boost your grade.

Knowledge check

Rapid-fire questions throughout the Content Guidance section to check your understanding.

Knowledge check answers

1 Turn to the back of the book for the Knowledge check answers.

Summaries

■ Each core topic is rounded off by a bullet-list summary for quick-check reference of what you need to know.

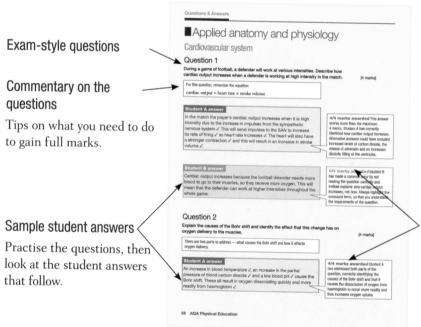

Exam-style questions

Commentary on the questions

Tips on what you need to do to gain full marks.

Sample student answers

Practise the questions, then look at the student answers that follow.

Commentary on sample student answers

Read the comments showing how many marks each answer would be awarded in the exam and exactly where marks are gained or lost.

■ About this book

This Student Guide covers the topics required for AQA A-level specification 7582 Paper 1: Factors affecting participation in physical activity and sport. Remember that this is a guide, not a textbook. It provides a succinct summary of what you need to know and understand for your exam, but is intended to complement, not replace, your textbook and class notes.

■ How to use the book

The first section, Content Guidance, follows the headings set out in the AQA specification. It is divided into three main topic areas:

■ Applied anatomy and physiology
■ Skill acquisition
■ Sport and society

To help aid your revision, each topic area in the Content Guidance includes exam tips, knowledge check questions and definitions of some key terms. Use the knowledge checks as you progress through the guide to test your understanding, and take on board the exam tips to avoid falling into the traps that most commonly result in students losing marks. At the end of each topic area there is a summary of the content covered. If you are unable to offer a detailed explanation of any part of this, you should work through this section again to clear up any misunderstanding.

The second section, Questions & Answers, begins by setting out the format of the exam papers, giving you advice and important tips on how to maximise your marks on the different elements of the paper. It also explains the levels system used for extended questions.

This is followed by a series of sample questions. These are all accompanied by example student answers, some illustrating best practice with others showing how *not* to answer the questions. You should attempt all of these questions yourself and compare your answers with the examples, while reading the detailed comments to help improve your understanding of what is required to achieve top marks.

Content Guidance

■ Applied anatomy and physiology

Cardiovascular system

The impact of physical activity and sport on the health of the individual

In terms of health, you need to know how physical activity can have an impact on coronary heart disease, high blood pressure, cholesterol levels and stroke. Regular physical activity has a positive effect on heart disease because it keeps the heart healthy and more efficient. It lowers 'bad' LDL cholesterol levels and significantly increases 'good' HDL cholesterol levels. It can also lower blood pressure by up to 5–10 mmHg and help you maintain a healthy weight, which can reduce your risk of stroke by 27%.

The impact of physical activity and sport on the fitness of the individual

Stroke volume

Stroke volume (SV) is the volume of blood pumped out by the heart ventricles in each contraction. On average, resting stroke volume is approximately 70 ml, but this value is much bigger in elite performers. SV increases as exercise intensity increases but only up to 40–60% of maximum effort. Once a performer reaches this point, SV plateaus because the ventricles do not have as much time to fill up with blood due to an increased heart rate (HR).

Starling's law explains how stroke volume increases during exercise. This occurs when there is an increase in venous return, which leads to a greater diastolic filling, so the cardiac muscle is stretched. Consequently, a more powerful force of contraction takes place, which increases the **ejection fraction** and therefore increases stroke volume.

Heart rate

Heart rate is the number of times the heart beats per minute. It increases with exercise — the higher the intensity, the higher the heart rate (Figure 1). Maximum heart rate can be calculated as 220 minus age.

A trained performer has a greater heart rate range because their resting heart rate is lower and maximum heart rate increases. Regular exercise causes hypertrophy of the heart, resulting in an increase in stroke volume and maximum cardiac output, leading to bradycardia (a lower resting heart rate of below 60 beats per minute).

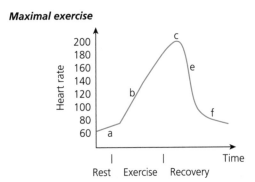

Maximal exercise

a = *Anticipatory rise* due to hormonal action of adrenaline which causes the SAN to increase heart rate

b = *Sharp rise* in heart rate due mainly to anaerobic work

c = Heart rate continues to rise due to maximal workloads stressing the anaerobic systems

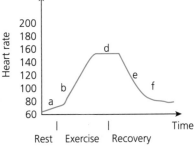

Submaximal exercise

d = *Steady state* as the athlete is able to meet the oxygen demand with the oxygen supply

e = *Rapid decline* in heart rate as soon as the exercise stops

f = *Slower recovery* as body systems return to resting levels; heart rate needs to remain elevated to rid the body of waste products, for example lactic acid

Figure 1 Heart rate responses to maximal and submaximal exercise

Cardiac output

Cardiac output, Q, is the amount of blood pumped out by each ventricle per minute, where:

$$Q = SV \times HR$$

Cardiac output stays the same at rest for both a trained and untrained performer. During exercise, maximum cardiac output increases due to an increase in HR and in SV. Cardiac output will increase as the intensity of exercise increases until maximum intensity is reached, and then it plateaus. During exercise the increase in maximum cardiac output will have huge benefits for the trained performer because they will be able to transport more blood, and therefore more oxygen, to the working muscles.

The hormonal, neural and chemical regulation of responses during physical activity and sport

Cardiac conduction system

Heart muscle is described as being myogenic because the beat originates in the heart muscle itself, with an electrical signal in the **SAN**. From the SAN the electrical impulse spreads through the walls of the atria causing them to contract (atrial systole). The impulse then passes through the AVN, where it is delayed for approximately 0.1 seconds to enable the atria to fully contract. The impulse then travels through the bundle of His, which divides into two branches and into the Purkinje fibres, which spread the impulse throughout the ventricles, causing them to contract (ventricular systole).

Knowledge check 3

How does regular training affect cardiac output, stroke volume and heart rate?

Exam tip

Remember that resting cardiac output is the same for both a trained and untrained performer. It is maximum cardiac output that is higher in a trained performer.

The **SAN** is a small mass of cardiac muscle found in the wall of the right atrium that generates the heart beat. It is more commonly called the pacemaker.

Knowledge check 4

How does the SAN control heart rate?

Factors affecting the change in rate of the conduction system

The conduction system ensures that HR increases during exercise to allow the working muscles to receive more oxygen. The rate at which impulses are fired from the SAN can be controlled by both neural and hormonal control mechanisms.

Neural control mechanism

This involves the sympathetic nervous system, which stimulates the heart to beat faster, and the parasympathetic nervous system, which returns the heart to its resting level. These two systems are coordinated by the cardiac control centre located in the **medulla oblongata** of the brain.

The cardiac control centre is stimulated by chemoreceptors, baroreceptors and proprioceptors, and then sends an impulse through either the sympathetic system to the SAN to increase HR or the parasympathetic system to the SAN to decrease HR.

 chemoreceptors detect increase in blood carbon dioxide → cardiac control centre → sympathetic system → SAN increases in HR

 baroreceptors detect increase in blood pressure → cardiac control centre → parasympathetic system → SAN decreases in HR

 proprioceptors detect increase in muscle movement → cardiac control centre → sympathetic system → SAN increases HR

Hormonal control mechanism

Adrenaline is a stress hormone that is released as a result of signals from the sympathetic nerves and cardiac nerves during exercise. It stimulates the SAN (pacemaker) which results in an increase in both the speed and force of contraction, therefore increasing cardiac output.

Cardiovascular drift

Cardiovascular drift refers to an increase in HR accompanied by a decrease in SV (Figure 2). It occurs after 10 minutes in warm conditions and is caused by a reduction of fluid in the blood plasma due to an increase in sweating. The blood becomes more viscous and, consequently, venous return decreases, so HR increases to maintain cardiac output.

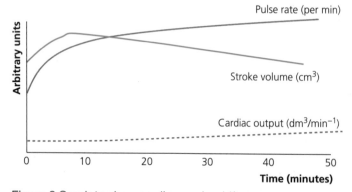

Figure 2 Graph to show cardiovascular drift

The **medulla oblongata** is the most important part of the brain because it regulates mechanisms that keep us alive.

Exam tip

The sympathetic system speeds up HR and the parasympathetic system slows it down.

Knowledge check 5

How does an increase in blood carbon dioxide affect heart rate?

Adrenaline is a stress hormone that stimulates the SAN.

Characteristics of blood vessels

- Veins — thinner muscle/elastic tissue layers, blood is at low pressure, valves are present and a wider lumen.
- Arteries — experience the highest pressure (and consequently have more of an elastic outer layer to cope with these fluctuations in pressure), a narrower lumen and a smooth inner layer.
- Capillaries have characteristics that help gaseous exchange. They are one cell thick, so there is a short diffusion pathway, have a large surface area and a narrow diameter to slow blood flow down. Training increases capillary density.

Exam tip

Make sure that you can explain why each type of blood vessel has the characteristics listed.

Blood pressure

Blood pressure is blood flow multiplied by resistance; an average reading is 120/80 mmHg. The top value is systolic pressure (ventricles contracting). The bottom value is diastolic pressure (ventricles relaxing). Blood pressure is highest in the arteries and lowest in the capillaries. Systolic pressure increases during aerobic exercise due to an increase in cardiac output, while diastolic pressure remains constant.

Venous return

During exercise, **venous return** increases. Active mechanisms are needed to help venous return:

- The skeletal muscle pump — when muscles contract and relax they press on nearby veins, causing a pumping effect and squeezing the blood towards the heart.
- The respiratory pump — when muscles contract and relax during the inspiration and expiration process, pressure changes occur in the thoracic and abdominal cavities. These pressure changes compress the nearby veins and assist blood return back to the heart.
- Valves — prevent the back flow of blood.
- A thin layer of smooth muscle within the veins helps squeeze blood back towards the heart.
- Gravity helps the blood return to the heart from the upper body.

Venous return is the return of blood back to the right side of the heart via the vena cava.

The impact of blood pressure on venous return

When systolic blood pressure increases, venous return increases because the pressure in the blood vessels is higher, causing the blood to travel more quickly. When systolic pressure decreases, venous return decreases because the pressure in the various blood vessels has dropped, causing blood flow to reduce.

Venous return is determined by a pressure gradient:

$$\frac{\text{venous pressure } (P_V) - \text{right atrial pressure } (P_{RA})}{\text{venous vascular resistance } (R_V)}$$

To simplify this:
- Increasing right atrial pressure decreases venous return.
- Decreasing right atrial pressure increases venous return.

Transportation of oxygen

Most of our transported oxygen (97%) combines with haemoglobin (an iron-containing pigment found in red blood cells) to form oxyhaemoglobin. The rest (3%) dissolves in the plasma. Training increases levels of haemoglobin.

Myoglobin, also known as 'muscle haemoglobin', acts as a store of oxygen in the muscle fibres, which can be used quickly during exercise. Training also increases levels of myoglobin.

Oxyhaemoglobin dissociation curve

The oxyhaemoglobin dissociation curve represents the relationship between oxygen and haemoglobin (Figure 3). From this curve you can see that in the lungs there is almost full saturation (concentration) of haemoglobin, but at the tissues (muscles) the partial pressure of oxygen is lower because haemoglobin gives up some of its oxygen to the muscles and is therefore no longer fully saturated.

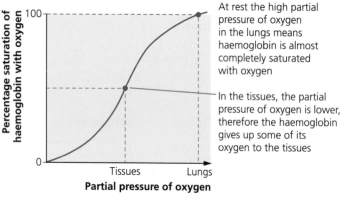

Figure 3 The oxyhaemoglobin dissociation curve

During exercise this S-shaped curve shifts to the right because, when muscles require more oxygen, the dissociation of oxygen from haemoglobin in the blood capillaries to the muscle tissue occurs more readily. This shift to the right is known as the **Bohr shift** (Figure 4). It is caused by three factors:

- a decrease in blood pH
- an increase in blood temperature
- an increase in blood CO_2

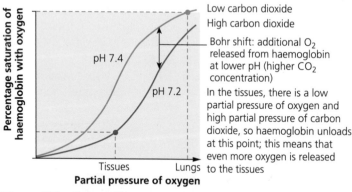

Figure 4 The Bohr shift

Knowledge check 6

What is the difference between haemoglobin and myoglobin?

Redistribution of blood (vascular shunt)

Both blood pressure and blood flow are controlled by the vasomotor centre, located in the medulla oblongata of the brain. During exercise chemical changes, such as increases in carbon dioxide and lactic acid, are detected by chemoreceptors. These receptors send impulses to the vasomotor centre, which redistributes blood flow through sympathetic stimulation. An increase in sympathetic stimulation causes **vasoconstriction** and a decrease in stimulation by the sympathetic nerves causes **vasodilation**.

During exercise more oxygen is needed at the working muscles, so vasodilation will occur in the arterioles supplying these muscles to increase blood flow. Vasoconstriction will occur in the arterioles supplying non-essential organs such as the intestines and liver.

Pre-capillary sphincters also aid blood redistribution. These are tiny rings of muscle located at the openings of capillaries. These relax around the muscles during exercise to increase blood flow and saturate the muscles with oxygen.

Redistribution of blood is important to:

- increase the supply of oxygen to the working muscles
- remove waste products from the muscles, such as a carbon dioxide and lactic acid
- ensure that more blood goes to the skin during exercise to regulate body temperature and get rid of heat through radiation, evaporation and sweating
- direct more blood to the heart, because it is a muscle and requires extra oxygen during exercise

Vasoconstriction is the narrowing of the blood vessels to reduce blood flow.

Vasodilation is the widening of the blood vessels to increase blood flow.

Arterio-venous oxygen difference (A-VO$_2$ diff)

This is the difference between the oxygen content of the arterial blood arriving at the muscles and the venous blood leaving the muscles. During exercise the **arterio-venous oxygen difference** is high. Consequently, at the alveoli more oxygen is taken in and more carbon dioxide removed. Training also increases the arterio-venous difference as trained performers can extract a greater amount of oxygen from the blood.

The **arterio-venous oxygen difference** is the difference between the oxygen content of the arterial blood arriving at the muscles and the venous blood leaving the muscles.

Summary

After studying this topic you should be able to:

- describe the cardiac conduction system
- explain the hormonal, neural and chemical regulation of the heart
- describe the role of chemoreceptors, baroreceptors and proprioceptors
- understand the impact of physical activity and sport on cardiac output, stroke volume and heart rate, and explain the relationship between them in trained/untrained individuals and during maximal/submaximal exercise
- understand Starling's law of the heart
- identify how physical activity can affect heart disease, high blood pressure, cholesterol levels and stroke
- explain cardiovascular drift
- understand the venous return mechanisms
- explain blood pressure using the terms systolic and diastolic, and identify the relationship venous return has with blood pressure
- describe the transportation of oxygen, and be able to explain the roles of haemoglobin and myoglobin
- understand the oxyhaemoglobin dissociation curve
- explain the Bohr shift
- explain how blood is redistributed during exercise through vasoconstriction and vasodilation
- explain arterio-venous oxygen difference (A-VO$_2$ diff)

Respiratory system

Lung volumes

For your exam you need to be able to define each of the lung volumes listed in Table 1 and explain what happens to them during exercise.

Table 1 The different components of an individual's total lung volume, and the changes that take place in these volumes during exercise

Lung volume or capacity	Definition	Change during exercise
Tidal volume	Volume of air breathed in or out per breath	Increase — allows more oxygen and carbon dioxide to be exchanged in the alveoli and an increase in oxygen delivery to the muscles
Inspiratory reserve volume	Volume of air that can be forcibly inspired after a normal breath	Decrease
Expiratory reserve volume	Volume of air that can be forcibly expired after a normal breath	Slight decrease
Residual volume	Volume of air that remains in the lungs after maximum expiration	Remains the same
Minute ventilation	Volume of air breathed in or out per minute	Big increase — see tidal volume above for how this increase helps maintain performance

The volume of air we breathe in and out can be measured using a spirometer; from this we get a spirometer trace. Each of the lung volumes can be labelled on a spirometer trace (Figure 5).

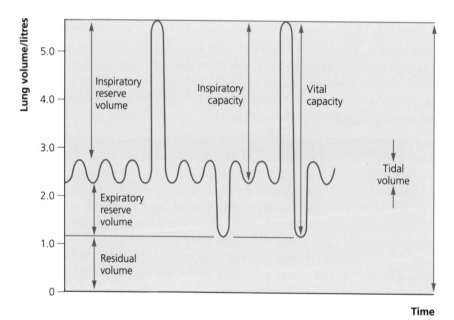

Figure 5 Spirometer trace of respiratory air

Exam tip

As well as being able to define these lung volumes, make sure that you are aware of their impact on physical activity and sport.

Knowledge check 7

What do you think would happen to a graphical representation of tidal volume and residual volume during exercise?

Gas exchange systems at the alveoli and muscles

Gaseous exchange at the alveoli

The structure of alveoli is designed to help gaseous exchange:

- Thin walls create a short **diffusion** pathway.
- Extensive capillary network surrounding the alveoli result in an excellent blood supply.
- A huge surface area, as a result of the millions of alveoli in each lung, allows for a greater uptake of oxygen.

The **partial pressure** of oxygen (pO_2) in the alveoli is higher than the partial pressure of oxygen in the capillary blood vessels. This is because oxygen has been removed by the working muscles, so its concentration in the blood is lower and therefore so is its partial pressure. The difference in partial pressure is referred to as the concentration/diffusion gradient; the bigger this gradient, the faster diffusion will be.

Oxygen will diffuse from the alveoli into the blood until the pressure is equal in both. The movement of carbon dioxide occurs in the same way, but in the reverse direction. This time the partial pressure of carbon dioxide (pCO_2) in the blood entering the alveolar capillaries is higher than in the alveoli, so carbon dioxide diffuses into the alveoli from the blood until the pressure is equal in both.

Gaseous exchange at the muscles

In the capillary membranes surrounding the muscle the partial pressure of oxygen is higher than in the muscle, which allows oxygen to diffuse from the blood into the muscle until equilibrium is reached. Conversely, the partial pressure of carbon dioxide in the blood is lower than in the muscle, so again diffusion occurs and carbon dioxide moves into the blood to be transported to the lungs.

Neural and chemical regulation of pulmonary ventilation during physical activity and sport

The sympathetic nervous system increases breathing rate and the parasympathetic nervous system lowers breathing rate. The respiratory centre located in the medulla oblongata of the brain controls the rate and depth of breathing, and uses both neural and chemical control. The respiratory centre has two main areas: the inspiratory centre is responsible for inspiration and expiration; the expiratory centre stimulates the expiratory muscles during exercise.

During exercise blood acidity increases due to an increase in both the plasma concentration of carbon dioxide and lactic acid production. These changes are detected by chemoreceptors, which send impulses to the inspiratory centre to increase ventilation until blood acidity has returned to normal. To achieve this, the respiratory centre sends impulses down the phrenic nerve to stimulate more inspiratory muscles: namely the sternocleidomastoid, scalenes and pectoralis minor. As a result, the rate, depth and rhythm of breathing increase.

Stretch receptors are activated when breathing is deeper, which occurs during exercise when the lungs are stretched more. Stretch receptors prevent over-inflation of the lungs by sending impulses to the expiratory centre and then down the intercostal nerve to the expiratory muscles (abdominals and internal intercostals), so that expiration occurs.

Diffusion is the movement of gas molecules from an area of high concentration or partial pressure to an area of low concentration or partial pressure.

Partial pressure is the pressure exerted by an individual gas when it exists within a mixture of gases.

Knowledge check 8

Explain how the gas exchange system operates at the muscles.

Role of proprioceptors and baroreceptors in the regulation of pulmonary ventilation

- Proprioceptors — these detect an increase in muscle movement and provide feedback to the respiratory centre to increase breathing during exercise.
- Baroreceptors — a decrease in blood pressure detected by baroreceptors in the aorta and carotid arteries results in an increase in breathing rate.

Impact of physical activity on the respiratory system

Taking part in physical activity and sport, as part of a healthy lifestyle, can have a positive effect on the respiratory system:

- It improves the efficiency of the respiratory system due to an increase in the surface area of alveoli and capillary density at the alveoli, so the body can supply muscles with more oxygen.
- Respiratory muscles are strengthened, resulting in deeper breathing.
- Greater gaseous exchange takes place, so more oxygen diffuses into blood and more carbon dioxide diffuses from the blood.
- Tidal volume and minute ventilation will increase, allowing more oxygen to diffuse into the blood and more carbon dioxide to diffuse into the alveoli.

Impact of poor lifestyle choices on the respiratory system

Lifestyle choices such as a poor diet, lack of physical activity, smoking and too much alcohol can all have a negative impact on the respiratory system.

Impact of smoking on the respiratory system

Smoking affects oxygen transport because the carbon monoxide from cigarettes combines with haemoglobin in red blood cells much more readily than oxygen. This reduces the oxygen-carrying capacity of the blood, which reduces the ability to work aerobically. This means that the performer will fatigue more quickly because more anaerobic respiration occurs. Smoking can also cause:

- irritation of the trachea and bronchi
- reduced lung function and increased breathlessness, caused by the swelling and narrowing of the lungs' airways
- damage to the cells lining the airways from cigarette smoke, leading to a build-up of excess mucus in the lungs and resulting in a smoker's cough, in an attempt to get rid of the mucus
- reduction in the efficiency of gaseous exchange and an increase in the risk of COPD (chronic obstructive pulmonary disease)

Knowledge check 9

Explain the impact of smoking on an endurance performer.

Summary

After studying this topic you should be able to:
- understand the following lung volumes: residual volume, expiratory reserve volume, inspiratory reserve volume, tidal volume and minute ventilation
- understand the impact of physical activity and sport on these lung volumes
- explain gas exchange of oxygen and carbon dioxide at alveoli and muscles, through the principles of diffusion and partial pressures
- understand the neural and chemical regulation of pulmonary ventilation during physical activity
- explain the role of chemoreceptors, proprioceptors and baroreceptors in the regulation of pulmonary ventilation during exercise
- understand the effect of physical activity and poor lifestyle choices on the respiratory system

Neuromuscular system

The role of the sympathetic and parasympathetic nervous systems

The sympathetic and parasympathetic nervous systems transmit information from the brain to the parts of the body that need to adjust what they are doing in order to prepare for or recover from exercise:

■ The **sympathetic nervous system** prepares the body for exercise and is often referred to as the 'fight-or-flight response'.

■ The **parasympathetic nervous system** relaxes the body and slows down many high-energy functions. It is often explained by the phrase 'rest and relax'.

> The **sympathetic nervous system** fires up the body for exercise.
>
> The **parasympathetic nervous system** slows everything down.

The characteristics and functions of the three muscle fibre types

Type I are slow-twitch fibres. These are better adapted to low-intensity, long-duration exercise. They produce their energy aerobically and have specific characteristics that allow them to use oxygen more effectively.

Type II are fast-twitch fibres and can generate a greater force of contraction. They produce most of their energy anaerobically. Type IIa fibres (fast oxidative glycolytic) are more resistant to fatigue and are used for events such as the 1500 m in athletics, where a longer burst of energy is needed. Type IIx (fast glycolytic) fibres fatigue quickly and are used for highly explosive events such as 100 m in athletics or power lifting. Table 2 highlights the characteristics and functions of the three fibre types.

> **Exam tip**
>
> Slow-twitch fibres are aerobic and fast-twitch fibres are anaerobic.

Table 2 The characteristics and functions of the three fibre types

Structural characteristic	Type I	Type IIa	Type IIx
Motor neurone size	Small	Large	Large
Mitochondrial density	High	Medium	Low
Myoglobin content	High	Medium	Low
Capillary density	High	Medium	Low
PC and glycogen store	Low	High	High
Function			
Contraction speed (milliseconds)	Slow (110)	Fast (50)	Fast (50)
Motor neurone conduction capacity	Slow	Fast	Fast
Force produced	Low	High	High
Fatiguability	Low	Medium	High
Aerobic capacity	Very high	Medium	Low
Anaerobic capacity	Low	High	Very high
Myosin ATPase/glycolytic enzyme activity	Low	High	Very high

> **Exam tip**
>
> Make sure you know which type of fibre is linked to which sporting activity.

> **Knowledge check 10**
>
> Which type of muscle fibre is linked to endurance?

The recruitment of muscle fibres using motor units to provide maximal contractions

Muscle fibres are grouped into motor units. A **motor unit** comprises a motor neurone and its muscle fibres. Each muscle is made up of many motor units and these vary in size. A small muscle that is used for fine motor control has small motor units; a large muscle used for gross motor control has large motor units.

Motor units contain the same type of muscle fibre, so they are either slow-twitch or fast-twitch motor units. To achieve maximal contraction, we need to use large motor

> A **motor unit** comprises a motor neurone and its muscle fibres.

units containing fast-twitch fibres and recruit lots of these motor units. We also need to ensure that the following takes place:

- The sequence of impulses has to be of sufficient intensity to stimulate all of the muscle fibres in a motor unit in order for them to contract, i.e. the all-or-none law is fulfilled.
- Wave summation — where there is a repeated nerve impulse with no time to relax, so a smooth, sustained contraction occurs rather than twitches.
- Tetanic contraction — a sustained, powerful muscle contraction caused by a series of fast-repeating stimuli.
- Spatial summation — where the strength of a contraction changes by altering the number and size of the muscle motor units used.

Exam tip

Questions on motor units often ask how a strong contraction can be achieved or how a performer can vary the strength of contraction.

The role of muscle spindles and Golgi tendon organs in PNF

Muscle spindles are proprioceptors that send excitory signals to the CNS about how far and how fast a muscle is being stretched. The CNS then sends impulses to the muscle to cause it to contract and produce the stretch reflex.

Golgi tendon organs detect levels of tension in a muscle. When the muscle is contracted isometrically in proprioceptive neuromuscular facilitation (PNF), they sense the increase in muscle tension and send inhibitory signals to the brain, which allows the antagonist muscle to relax and lengthen. This is known as **autogenic inhibition**.

Autogenic inhibition is where there is a sudden relaxation of the muscle in response to high tension.

PNF in practice

The individual performs a passive stretch of the hamstrings until tension is felt. This stretch is detected by the muscle spindles. If the muscle is being stretched too far then a stretch reflex occurs (Figure 6a).

The individual then isometrically contracts the muscle for at least 10 seconds by pushing their leg against their partner, who supplies just enough resistance to hold the leg in a stationary position. Golgi tendon organs are sensitive to tension developed in a muscle and during an isometric contraction they are activated and the inhibitory signals they send override the excitatory signals from the muscle spindles, therefore delaying the stretch reflex (Figure 6b).

As the leg is passively stretched again, the Golgi tendon organs are responsible for the antagonist muscle relaxing which means the leg stretches further. This process can be repeated until no more gains are possible (Figure 6c).

Knowledge check 11

When are muscle spindles activated in a muscle?

Knowledge check 12

When are Golgi tendon organs activated in a muscle?

(a)  (b)  (c)

Figure 6 PNF in practice

Summary

After studying this topic you should be able to:

■ understand the role of the sympathetic and parasympathetic nervous systems
■ identify the characteristics and functions of the three fibre types: slow-twitch (type I), fast oxidative glycolytic (type IIa) and fast glycolytic (type IIx) for a variety of sporting activities
■ explain the recruitment of muscle fibres through an explanation of motor units
■ explain the terms spatial summation, wave summation, all-or-none law and tetanic contraction
■ describe the role of the two proprioceptors — muscle spindles and Golgi tendon organs — in PNF

The musculoskeletal system and analysis of movement in physical activities

Type of joint and articulating bones of the ankle, knee, hip, shoulder and elbow

Table 3 lists the above joints, along with their types and **articulating bones**.

Table 3 Joints, types and their articulating bones

Joint	Joint type	Articulating bones
Elbow	Hinge	Radius, ulna, humerus
Shoulder	Ball and socket	Scapula, humerus
Hip	Ball and socket	Pelvis, femur
Knee	Hinge	Femur, tibia
Ankle	Hinge	Talus, tibia, fibula

Articulating bones are bones that meet and move at a joint.

Planes and axes

There are three planes and axes you need to know:

■ Flexion, extension, plantar flexion, dorsi flexion and hyperextension occur in a sagittal plane about a transverse axis (Figure 7). A sagittal plane divides the body into right and left halves and a transverse axis runs from side to side across the body.
■ Horizontal abduction and horizontal adduction occur in a transverse plane about a longitudinal axis (Figure 8). A transverse plane divides the body into upper and lower halves and a longitudinal axis runs from top to bottom.
■ Abduction and adduction occur in a frontal plane about a sagittal axis (Figure 9). A frontal plane divides the body into front and back halves and a sagittal axis runs from front to back.

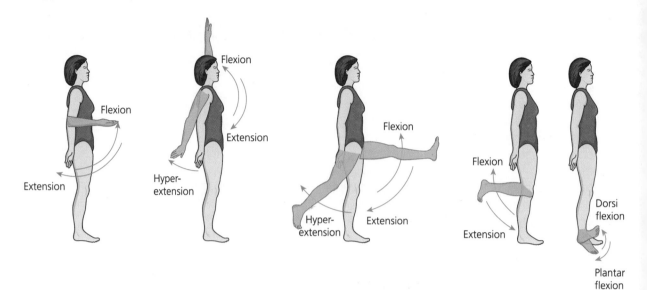

Figure 7 The joint actions occurring in a sagittal plane and transverse axis: flexion and extension at the elbow, shoulder, hip and knee, and plantar flexion and dorsi flexion in the ankle

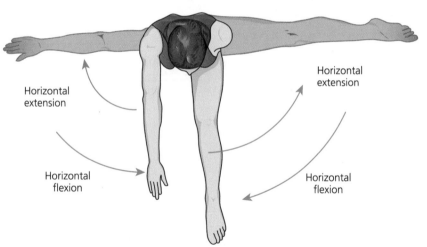

Figure 8 Horizontal abduction and adduction take place in the hip and shoulder in a transverse plane about a longitudinal axis

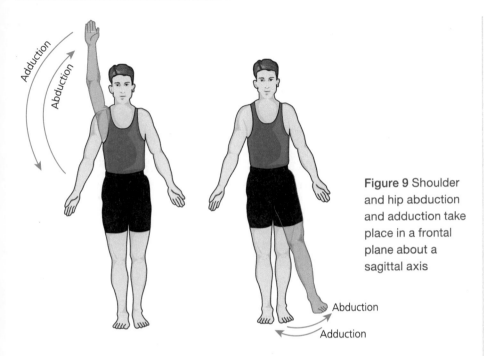

Figure 9 Shoulder and hip abduction and adduction take place in a frontal plane about a sagittal axis

Exam tip

Practise labelling the examined joint actions on various sporting pictures.

Agonists and antagonists

You need to learn the main agonists and antagonists for each of the joint actions (Table 4).

Table 4 Joint actions and their agonists and antagonists

Joint action	Agonist	Antagonist
Elbow flexion	Biceps	Triceps
Elbow extension	Triceps	Biceps
Ankle plantar flexion	Gastrocnemius	Tibialis anterior
Ankle dorsi flexion	Tibialis anterior	Gastrocnemius
Knee flexion	Hamstrings	Quadriceps
Knee extension	Quadriceps	Hamstrings
Hip flexion	Hip flexors	Gluteals
Hip extension/hyperextension	Gluteals	Hip flexors
Hip adduction	Adductors	Gluteus medius/minimus
Hip abduction	Gluteus medius/minimus	Adductors
Hip horizontal adduction	Adductors/hip flexors	Gluteus medius/minimus
Hip horizontal abduction	Gluteus medius/minimus	Adductors/hip flexors
Shoulder flexion	Anterior deltoid	Latissimus dorsi
Shoulder extension/hyperextension	Latissimus dorsi	Anterior deltoid
Shoulder horizontal abduction	Latissimus dorsi	Pectorals
Shoulder horizontal adduction	Pectorals	Latissimus dorsi
Shoulder adduction	Latissimus dorsi	Middle deltoid
Shoulder abduction	Middle deltoid	Latissimus dorsi

Joint action	Hip abduction	
Plane and axis		
Agonist		Quadriceps
Antagonist		

Knowledge check 13

Copy and complete the blanks in the movement analysis table on the left.

Types of muscular contraction

An isotonic contraction is where the muscles are contracting and changing length — movement takes place. There are two types:

- Concentric contraction — when a muscle shortens under tension.
- Eccentric contraction — when a muscle lengthens under tension.

An isometric contraction is where the muscle is under tension but there is no visible movement.

Exam tip

In an eccentric contraction the muscle is acting as a brake.

Summary

After studying this topic you should be able to:
- identify the type of joint and articulating bones for the ankle, knee, hip, shoulder and elbow
- identify the following joint actions: flexion, extension, hyperextension, plantar flexion and dorsi flexion, abduction, adduction, horizontal abduction and horizontal adduction
- identify which plane and axis each of these joint actions occurs in
- state the main agonists and antagonists for the actions occurring at these joints
- explain the types of muscle contraction: isotonic (concentric and eccentric) and isometric

Energy systems

Adenosine triphosphate (ATP) is the energy we use for muscle contractions. We have to constantly rebuild ATP by converting ADP and Pi back into ATP using phosphocreatine, carbohydrates, fats and protein in one of three energy systems.

Adenosine triphosphate (ATP) is the only usable form of energy in the body.

Energy transfer during short duration/high intensity exercise

The ATP-PC system

The ATP-PC system provides energy for high-intensity activities lasting less than 10 seconds. The system is anaerobic and occurs in the sarcoplasm. Creatine kinase is the enzyme that breaks down the PC that is stored in the muscles into creatine and phosphate. Energy is released for ATP synthesis and aerobic energy is needed for recovery.

Knowledge check 14

What are the key points of the ATP-PC system?

Anaerobic glycolytic system

The anaerobic glycolytic system provides energy for high-intensity activity for longer than the ATP-PC system. How long this system lasts depends on the fitness of the individual and the intensity of the exercise. Working flat out to exhaustion means that the system will last a shorter time. This is because the demand for energy is extremely high. However, at a slightly lower intensity the system can last longer — up to 2–3 minutes — because the demand for energy is slightly lower.

The key points you need to know for this system are as follows:

- It is anaerobic and occurs in the sarcoplasm.
- PFK is the enzyme that is responsible for **glycolysis**.
- Glycogen is converted to glucose-6-phosphate and broken down to pyruvic acid.
- Pyruvic acid is then converted to lactic acid.
- 2 ATP are produced.

Lactate accumulation/OBLA

When the by-product lactic acid is produced as a result of glycolysis it quickly breaks down, releasing hydrogen ions (H^+). As lactate accumulates in the muscles, so do the hydrogen ions, and it is actually the presence of hydrogen ions that increases acidity. This slows down enzyme activity, which affects the breakdown of glycogen, causing muscle fatigue.

OBLA and **lactate threshold** can be used interchangeably. Lactate threshold is the point at which lactic acid rapidly accumulates in the blood, whereas OBLA is the point at which lactate levels go above 4 millimols per litre. Measuring OBLA gives an indication of endurance capacity. Some individuals can work at higher levels of intensity than others before OBLA.

Lactate threshold is expressed as a percentage of VO_2 max. As fitness increases, the lactate threshold becomes delayed. Average performers have a lower lactate threshold than elite performers and work at a much lower percentage of their VO_2 max. Elite power athletes have much better anaerobic endurance than non-elite performers. This is because their body has adapted to cope with higher levels of lactate. In addition, through a process called **buffering**, they are able to increase the rate of lactate removal and consequently have lower lactate levels.

Factors affecting the rate of lactate accumulation

- Intensity of exercise — the higher the intensity, the faster lactate accumulation occurs.
- Slow-twitch fibres produce less lactate than fast-twitch fibres.
- VO_2 max of a performer/buffering capacity — the higher the level, the more reduced the rate of lactate accumulation.
- A respiratory exchange ratio close to 1.0 means that glycogen becomes the preferred fuel and there is quicker lactate accumulation.
- Higher level of fitness of the performer/regular training — delays OBLA because adaptations occur in trained muscles, for example increased numbers of mitochondria and myoglobin, and greater capillary density.

Energy transfer during long-duration/lower-intensity exercise

The aerobic system

The aerobic system provides energy for low-intensity activities lasting longer than 1–2 minutes, and has three stages:

- Stage one — glycolysis (as above).
- Stage two — the Krebs cycle. The pyruvic acid produced in glycolysis splits into two acetyl groups, which are carried into the Krebs cycle by coenzyme A.

Glycolysis is the breakdown of glucose into pyruvic acid.

OBLA is the point at which lactate levels go above 4 millimoles per litre.

Lactate threshold is the point at which lactic acid rapidly accumulates in the blood.

Buffering is a process that aids the removal of lactate and maintains acidity levels in the blood and muscle.

Knowledge check 15

Identify three factors that affect the rate at which a performer accumulates lactic acid.

Acetyl coenzyme A diffuses into the matrix of the mitochondria and combines with oxaloacetic acid, forming citric acid. This is oxidised and CO_2 is removed. Hydrogen ions are formed and passed onto the electron transport chain, and 2 ATP are resynthesised. Fats can also enter the Krebs cycle after a process called beta oxidation has taken place, where fatty acids are broken down to acetyl coenzyme A.

■ Stage three — the electron transport chain occurs in the cristae of the mitochondria, water is formed and 34 ATP are resynthesised.

Energy continuum of physical activity

Energy continuum is a term that describes the type of respiration used by a physical activity (Figure 10). Whether it is aerobic or anaerobic respiration depends on the intensity and duration of the exercise (Table 5).

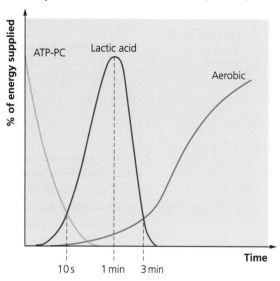

Figure 10 The energy continuum related to exercise duration

Table 5 Energy system used according to intensity and duration of exercise

Duration of performance	Intensity	Energy supplied by
Less than 10 seconds	Very high	ATP-PC
8–90 seconds	High–very high	ATP-PC and anaerobic glycolytic
90 seconds to 3 minutes	High	Anaerobic glycolytic and aerobic
3+ minutes	Low–medium	Aerobic

Knowledge check 16

Give an example, in a team game, of when each of the three energy systems is used.

Differences in ATP generation between slow- and fast-twitch fibres

Table 6 outlines the differences in ATP generation between slow- and fast-twitch fibres.

Table 6 Differences in ATP generation between slow- and fast-twitch fibres

Slow-twitch fibres (type I)	Fast-twitch fibres (type IIx)
Produce ATP aerobically	Produce ATP anaerobically
Produce up to 36 ATP per glucose molecule	Produce only 2 ATP per glucose molecule
Production is slow, but these fibres are more endurance-based and so less likely to fatigue	Production of ATP this way is fast, but cannot last for long because these fibres have the least resistance to muscle fatigue

Oxygen consumption during exercise (maximal and submaximal oxygen deficit)

Oxygen consumption is the amount of oxygen we *use* to produce ATP, whereas submaximal oxygen deficit is when there is not enough oxygen available at the start of exercise to provide all the energy (ATP) aerobically. Maximal oxygen deficit is usually referred to as maximal accumulated oxygen deficit, or MAOD. It gives an indication of anaerobic capacity.

Oxygen consumption during recovery (excess post-exercise oxygen consumption — EPOC)

EPOC is the amount of O_2 consumed during recovery above that which is normally consumed at rest. It is the breathlessness we experience when exercise is finished — the extra oxygen that is taken in is used to put things back to normal. That which can be returned to normal quickly is called the fast replenishment stage (alactacid component). This involves the restoration of ATP and PC, together with the resaturation of myoglobin with oxygen. Restoration of PC takes up to 3 minutes for 100%/30 seconds for 50% and uses 2–3 litres of oxygen. Myoglobin replenishment takes up to 2 minutes and uses 0.5 litres of oxygen.

The slow replenishment stage (lactacid component) involves the removal of lactic acid and can take an hour or more. It is achieved by oxidising lactic acid into carbon dioxide and water, and so is used as an energy source. Lactic acid can also be converted into glycogen, glucose and protein, and removed through sweat and urine. During this stage, heart rate, respiratory rate and body temperature remain elevated.

Knowledge check 17

What are the functions of the fast component?

VO₂ max

VO$_2$ max is the maximum volume of oxygen that can be taken up and used by the muscles per minute. A good VO$_2$ max allows a performer to work at a higher intensity for longer by utilising oxygen more effectively.

Factors affecting VO₂ max/aerobic power

The following structural/physiological characteristics will enable a performer to have a higher VO$_2$ max:

- increased maximum cardiac output
- increased stroke volume/ejection fraction/cardiac hypertrophy
- greater heart rate range
- increased levels of haemoglobin and red blood cell count
- increased stores of glycogen and triglycerides
- increased myoglobin content
- increased capillarisation around the muscles
- increased number and size of mitochondria
- increased surface area of alveoli
- increased lactate tolerance
- reduced body fat
- slow-twitch hypertrophy

Exam tip

Make sure that you can explain how these factors have an impact on VO$_2$ max.

The following general factors can also affect VO_2 max:

- Lifestyle — smoking, sedentary lifestyle, poor diet and fitness can all reduce VO_2 max.
- Training — VO_2 max can be improved by up to 10–20% following a period of aerobic training.
- Genetics — VO_2 max is largely genetically determined, which limits the impact of training.
- Gender — men generally have an approximately 20% higher VO_2 max than women.
- Age — as we get older, VO_2 max declines because our body systems become less efficient.
- Body composition — a higher percentage of body fat decreases VO_2 max.

Measurements of energy expenditure

- Indirect calorimetry measures how much carbon dioxide is produced and how much oxygen is consumed both at rest and during aerobic exercise. It is a reliable test because it gives a precise calculation of VO_2 and VO_2 max.
- Lactate sampling measures lactate levels in the blood and is an accurate and objective measure. It can measure exercise intensity, give an idea of level of fitness and enable the performer to select relevant training zones. It also provides a comparison to see whether improvement has occurred. If test results show an increase, this would indicate that the performer has improved peak speed/power, increased time to exhaustion, improved recovery heart rate and a higher lactate threshold.
- Respiratory exchange ratio is the ratio of carbon dioxide released *compared with* oxygen used by the body. It calculates energy expenditure and provides information about which energy source (fat or carbohydrate) is being oxidised, and hence whether the performer is working aerobically or anaerobically. An RER value close to 1 indicates that the performer is using carbohydrates; an RER value of approximately 0.7 means the performer is using fats; an RER value greater than 1 implies anaerobic respiration.
- VO_2 max tests, such as the mult-stage fitness test and the Cooper 12 minute run, only give an indication or prediction of VO_2 max. A sports science laboratory can produce much more valid and reliable results using **direct gas analysis**, which measures the concentration of oxygen that is inspired and the concentration of carbon dioxide that is expired, for example the treadmill test/cycle ergometer.

Direct gas analysis measures the concentration of oxygen that is inspired and the concentration of carbon dioxide that is expired.

Impact of specialist training methods on energy systems

- Altitude training (altitude starts to have an effect at around 1500 m above sea level but most athletes choose to train at 2500 m+). Here the partial pressure of oxygen is lower, so haemoglobin is not fully saturated, which lowers the oxygen-carrying capacity of the blood.
  - Advantages — increase in red blood cells, increased concentration of haemoglobin, increased blood viscosity and capillarisation, enhanced oxygen transport and increased lactate tolerance.
  - Disadvantages — expensive, altitude sickness, detraining because training intensity has to reduce when the performer first trains at altitude (due to the decreased availability of oxygen), benefits quickly lost on return to sea level, psychological (e.g. homesickness).

- High-intensity interval training (HIIT) involves short intervals of anaerobic maximum intensity exercise followed by a recovery interval of aerobic exercise.
- Plyometric training improves power/speed. It involves high-intensity explosive activities (e.g. jumping) and works on the principle that muscles can generate more force if they have previously been stretched. An eccentric contraction occurs first, followed by a concentric contraction (stretch-shortening cycle). It has three phases:
  1 Eccentric phase — on landing, the muscle performs an eccentric contraction, which stretches the muscle.
  2 Amortisation phase — the time between the eccentric and concentric muscle contractions. This time needs to be short so that the energy stored from the eccentric contraction is not lost.
  3 Concentric contraction phase — this uses the stored energy to increase the force of the contraction.
- Speed agility quickness (SAQ) training aims to improve multidirectional movement through developing the neuromuscular system, for example foot ladders. Activities are performed with maximum force at high speed, so energy is provided anaerobically.

Exam tip

As well as knowing each method of training, make sure that you can also evaluate their appropriateness for different types of performer.

Summary

After studying this topic you should be able to:
- explain how the anaerobic glycolytic and ATP-PC systems provide energy during short-duration/high-intensity exercise
- explain how the aerobic system provides energy during long-duration/low-intensity exercise
- understand the energy continuum and explain which energy system is the main energy provider according to the intensity and duration of exercise
- identify the difference in ATP production depending on the fibre type used
- understand the effects of using the anaerobic glycolytic energy system through an explanation of lactate accumulation, lactate threshold and OBLA
- explain oxygen consumption during exercise, and recovery through oxygen deficit and EPOC
- identify VO_2 max and explain the factors that affect it
- explain the measurements of energy expenditure, to include indirect calorimetry, lactate sampling, VO_2 max test and respiratory exchange ratio
- understand the impact of altitude training, high-intensity interval training, plyometric training and speed agility quickness on energy systems

Skill acquisition

Skill, skill continua and transfer of skills

Characteristics of skill

- A **skilful performer** will have worked very hard and practised repeatedly to achieve a high level of performance.
- Their skills are learned.
- They achieve a high success rate; they are accurate and consistent.
- They perform their skills with little effort and in the quickest time possible, making them efficient and economical.
- The skills are performed smoothly and fluently.
- Before starting a particular skill they will have a clear aim in mind, knowing exactly what they want to happen. The skill is goal directed.
- The skill looks good. It is attractive to watch, making it aesthetically pleasing.

Use of skill continua

A continuum is an imaginary sliding scale on which skills can be placed, between two extremes of a characteristic. Continua are used to classify skills. It is important to understand the characteristics of skills so that they can be taught, practised and perfected. You must have knowledge and understanding of six continua:

1 Open–closed

- **Open skills:** the environment is ever changing and unpredictable. The performer must adapt and make lots of decisions, for example passing in hockey.
- **Closed skills:** the environment is stable and predictable, allowing the performer to repeat the same movement pattern over and over without adjusting, for example a javelin throw.

2 Discrete–serial–continuous

- **Discrete skills:** have a clear beginning and ending, for example an overhead clear in badminton.
- **Serial skills:** comprise a number of discrete skills grouped together and performed in a specific order, for example grouping the hop, step and jump together as the triple jump.
- **Continuous skills:** do not have a clear beginning and ending. They are cyclic. The end of one skill becomes the beginning of the next, for example cycling.

3 Gross–fine

- **Gross skills:** performed using large muscle groups, for example an ice hockey tackle.
- **Fine skills:** performed using small muscle groups and requiring precision, accuracy and control, for example pistol shooting.

A **skilful performer** has the learned ability to bring about predetermined results with the minimum outlay of time, energy or both (*Skill in Sport: Attainment of Proficiency*, Barbara Knapp, 1963).

Exam tip

Remember to read and highlight the command term. Often questions on skilful performance will ask you to describe and/ or give examples of the characteristics, rather than just identify/outline/ list them.

Knowledge check 18

A skilful performer will be good to watch and fluent. What are the other characteristics of skill?

4 Self-paced–externally paced

- **Self-paced skills:** the performer controls the timing and speed of the skill, for example a free throw in basketball is taken with as much speed as the player wishes.
- **Externally paced skills:** the environment controls the timing and speed of the skill being performed, for example a kite surfer responding to wind speed and direction in order to gain big air.

5 High organisation–low organisation

- **High-organisation skills:** hard to break down into subroutines and practised individually. They are often ballistic, for example an overhead bicycle kick.
- **Low-organisation skills:** easy to separate into subroutines and practised individually, for example breast stroke.

6 Simple–complex

- **Simple skills:** few decisions are made when producing the skill, for example a leap in dance.
- **Complex skills:** several decisions are made when producing the skill, for example a pass in basketball.

Transfer of learning

Transfer explains the effect that the learning of a skill may have on another. Nearly all learning is based on some form of transfer:

- **Positive** — the learning and performance of a skill help the athlete to learn and perform another skill, for example learning the chest pass in basketball will assist in learning the netball chest pass.
- **Negative** — the learning and performance of a skill hinders the athlete when learning and performing another skill, for example learning the tennis backhand hinders the control when performing a badminton backhand.
- **Zero** — the learning and performance of one skill has no impact/effect on the learning and performance of another skill for example learning the front crawl has no effect when learning the volley in football.
- **Bilateral** — learning and performing a skill on one side of the body/limb leads to it being performed equally as well on the opposing side of the body/limb, for example someone who can dribble a basketball proficiently with her left hand practises dribbling with her right hand in order become equally competent on that side.

The impact of transfer of learning on skill development

Transfer can impact positively on skill development if:

- the coach highlights where positive transfer takes place
- the performer has overlearned the first skill before practising the second/more advanced skill
- the practice environment is close to the game situation
- the coach offers positive reinforcement when positive transfer occurs

Exam tip

Questions on classification regularly appear on exam papers. Focus clearly on the command term. If you are asked to *justify* your answer, i.e. give a reason, use 'because' in your answer and always support it with a practical example.

Exam tip

A common mistake is to use a question term in your answer, for example 'positive transfer is when the skill is affected positively'. The examiner will not award marks for this. Use a different word to describe 'positively'.

Summary

After studying this topic you should be able to:
- identify, describe and give examples of skilful performance
- name each classification of skill and support your classification with a clear practical example
- justify clearly your reasons for how you classify skills on each continuum
- identify, describe and give examples of the four types of transfer
- describe the impact that transfer can have on skill development

Impact of skill classification on structure of practice for learning

Methods of presentation

Whole

Description

Presenting the skill in its entirety. The skill is not broken down into parts/subroutines.

When to choose this method

The skill is:
- highly organised
- continuous/cyclic
- simple
- discrete
- fast/ballistic
- not dangerous

The performer is autonomous.

Advantages

- **Kinaesthesis** is developed.
- Fluency between subroutines is maintained.
- Not time consuming.
- Creates a clear mental image.
- Easily transferred into the full game.
- Aids understanding.

Kinaesthesis involves internal muscle feelings/intrinsic feedback.

Disadvantages

- Not ideal for cognitive performers.
- Can cause information overload.
- Can cause fatigue.
- Performer must be physically capable of producing the full skill.

Activities

Use this method with:
- golf swing
- cycling
- forward roll

Whole–part–whole

Description

The learner attempts the full skill, then one (or each) subroutine is practised in isolation until grooved, then integrated back into the entire skill.

When to choose this method

The skill is:

- complex
- fast/ballistic

The performer is:

- cognitive and is grooving individual parts
- autonomous and is concentrating on a specific weakness

Advantages

- Kinaesthesis is maintained in the whole.
- Weak parts/subroutines can be improved.
- Fluency between subroutines is maintained in the whole.
- Confidence and motivation increase as success is seen in each part.

Disadvantages

- Time consuming.
- Cannot be used with highly organised skills.
- Kinaesthesis/fluency can be negatively affected if the part is not integrated adequately and quickly.

Activities

Use this method with front crawl:

- Whole — introduce the full stroke; allow the performer to experience it entirely. Note that arm action is weak.
- Part — practise arm action in isolation with the aid of a pull buoy/floats until grooved.
- Whole — practise the stroke as one again, now with improved arm action.

Progressive part

Description

The first subroutine/part is taught and practised until perfected. The rest of the parts are then added sequentially until the whole of the skill can be performed. Sometimes called 'chaining'.

When to choose this method

The skill is:

- low organisation
- serial
- complex
- dangerous

The performer is cognitive.

Advantages

- Focusing on just one part of the skill reduces the chance of overload and fatigue.
- Aids understanding of each part.
- Confidence and motivation increase as success is seen in each part.
- Danger is reduced.

Disadvantages

- Very time consuming.
- Cannot use with highly organised skills.
- Fluency between subroutines can be negatively affected.
- Kinaesthesis/feel for whole skill not experienced until the very end.

Activities

Use this method with triple jump:

- Teach hop — practise until grooved.
- Teach step — practise until grooved.
- Practise hop and step together.
- Teach jump — practise until grooved.
- Practise hop, step and jump together.

Types of practice

Massed practice

Description

Continuous practice without rest periods.

When to choose this method

The skill is:

- discrete
- closed
- self-paced
- simple

The performers are:

- highly motivated
- autonomous
- physically fit

Advantages

- Grooves/overlearns skills so they become habitual.
- Motor programmes are formed.
- Improves fitness.

Disadvantages

- Causes fatigue.
- Performer may not be physically capable of undertaking the practice.
- No time for feedback.

Activities

Use this method with a badminton short serve. Perfect the shot by repeatedly performing the action without rest.

Distributed practice

Description

Practice with rest periods included.

When to choose this method

The skills are:

- continuous
- complex
- serial
- low organisation

- dangerous/tiring
- externally paced
- open

The performers are:

- cognitive
- unfit
- lacking motivation

Advantages

- More effective method than massed practice.
- Allows time for physical recovery.
- Allows time for mental practice (see below).

- Coach can give feedback.
- Motivational.

Disadvantages

- Time consuming.
- Can cause negative transfer.

Activities

Use this method with the steeplechase:

- Run part of the course during a training race, followed by a rest period.
- Mentally rehearse the run, visualising your stride pattern, as well as clearing the hurdles and water barrier.

Variable practice

Description

Practising skills and drills in a constantly changing environment.

When to choose this method

The skills are:

- open
- externally paced
- complex

The performers are:

- cognitive
- lacking motivation

Exam tip

Questions about presentation and/or practice types will require you to link them to skill classifications. Ensure you know which method is most useful for which type of skill.

Advantages
- Develops schema.
- Increases motivation.
- Performer gains experience in a range of situations.
- Positive transfer from training to game.

Disadvantages
- Time consuming.
- Can cause fatigue.
- Possibility of information overload.
- Can cause negative transfer.

Activities

Use this method when a netball goal attack practises shooting:
- The GA practises shooting on goal from a range of positions in the circle.
- She starts without a defender, then a passive GD is introduced and finally the GD is fully active.

Mental practice

Description

Going over the skill in your mind without moving:
- Internal — seeing your performance from 'within' through your own eyes.
- External — seeing your performance from outside as a spectator.

When to choose this method

The skills are:
- complex
- serial

The performers are:
- cognitive — to build a clear mental image of the basics of the skill
- autonomous — to focus on key strategies/tactics

Advantages
- Produces a clear mental image.
- Performer can see themselves being successful.
- Can rehearse strategies/tactics.
- Increases confidence.
- Reduces anxiety.
- Muscles are stimulated.
- Reaction time improves.

Disadvantages
- Difficult for cognitive performers to complete effectively.
- Mental image must be accurate.
- Difficult if environment is not quiet.

Activities

Use this method with the high jump. A high jumper about to take their final jump in a competition visualises the run up, execution and landing of the jump before starting to perform.

Exam tip

When answering questions on presentation/practice, be careful not to use the question terms in your answer. For example, instead of saying whole presentation means producing the skill as a whole, refer to the full skill or the skill in its entirety. Likewise, with varied practice, refer to changing the skill situation, not varying the drills.

Knowledge check 19

What is the difference between massed and distributed practice?

Knowledge check 20

What types of skill would you use progressive part presentation with?

Summary

After studying this topic you should be able to:
- describe each of the types of presentation and suggest with which classification of skill it would be used most effectively
- describe each of the types of practice and suggest with which classification of skill it would be used most effectively
- give practical examples to support your answers

Principles and theories of learning and performance

Stages of learning

Table 7 show the three stages of learning.

Table 7 The three stages of learning

1 The cognitive stage	2 The associative stage	3 The autonomous stage
Mental image created	Continue practising	Fluent, efficient movements
Demonstration necessary	Some performers never progress out of this	Skills are executed automatically
Mental rehearsal required	stage	without conscious thought
Many mistakes	Fewer mistakes	Motor programmes fully formed
Trial-and-error learning	Smoother movements	Focus on fine detail, tactics and
Jerky movements	Begin to focus on the finer aspects of the	advanced strategies
All attention on the skill	skill	Practice and mental rehearsal
Motor programmes not formed	Motor programmes are developing	required to stay at this level
Feedback:	Demonstrations, positive feedback and	**Feedback:**
■ Reliant on extrinsic feedback	mental rehearsal still needed	■ Internal kinaesthesis used to
■ Positive feedback maintains	**Feedback:**	correct own mistakes
motivation	■ Internal kinaesthesis develops	■ Extrinsic feedback used to
■ Some knowledge of results can	■ Extrinsic feedback is still used to refine	correct errors
be used	actions	■ Knowledge of performance used
	■ Begin to use knowledge of performance	readily

Learning plateau

A typical learning curve illustrates the rate of improvement shown by a performer when learning a new, closed skill (Figure 11). The **plateau** is a period during the performance when there are no signs of improvement.

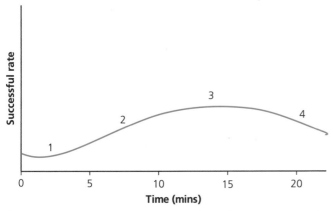

Figure 11 A learning curve, showing rate of improvement when attempting a closed skill over a 20-minute period

Exam tip

Do not confuse the cognitive stage of learning with the cognitive theory of learning.

Knowledge check 21

What type of feedback is used by a cognitive performer?

The **plateau** is a steady state during which no further learning occurs.

The learning curve illustrates the stages a performer goes though when learning a new, closed skill (Table 8).

Table 8 Stages of learning a new skill

Stage 1	Stage 2	Stage 3	Stage 4
■ Low success rate ■ Slow, jerky movements ■ Developing an understanding	■ Sharp increase in success rate ■ Increased fluency ■ High motivation	■ Plateau reached ■ Progress halted ■ Performance levels maintained	■ Reduced success rate ■ Motivation reduced ■ Experiencing drive reduction ■ New challenge/goal needed

Causes and solutions

The plateau can be caused by a number of reasons. Table 9 shows some of these causes, together with possible solutions.

Table 9 Causes and solutions for the learning plateau

Causes	Solutions
Loss of motivation/boredom	Set new tasks/challenges Use variable practice Offer tangible rewards
Mental/physical fatigue	Allow the performer to rest Use distributed practice
Have reached ability limit	Allow performer to compete against others of similar ability
Poor coaching	Try a variety of coaching methods Try an alternative coach
Incorrect goals set	Set goals using the SMARTER principle

Theories of learning

Psychologists have suggested various theories of how individuals learn. Their theories can be applied to learning skills in sport. Four of these theories are outlined below.

Cognitive theories: insight learning (Gestalt)

- Learn skills through experiencing the *whole* task.
- Part learning is not effective.
- *Kinaesthesis* and the *flow* of the skill are maintained.
- Greater *understanding* — the coach poses *questions* that the performer answers.
- They use their *insight* and *adapt* to the sporting situation.
- Allows performers to be *creative* and *develop their own strategies and tactics*.

Behaviourism: operant conditioning (Skinner)

- Learn by creating a *link/association* between a *stimulus* and a *response*. This is known as an **S–R bond**.
- Use **trial-and-error learning**.
- Manipulate the environment.
- Offer positive reinforcement when a correct response is given.
- Behaviour is shaped.

Other strategies used to shape behaviour include:

- **Positive reinforcement** — endorsing a correct action so that it will be repeated.

Exam tip

When describing the learning curve, do not just focus on the shape of the curve — link it directly to the performer and how they are developing.

Knowledge check 22

Describe stage 2 of the learning curve.

The **S–R bond** is the link/relationship between a stimulus and a response.

Trial-and-error learning is where a performer attempts various methods of performing a skill. If/when they are unsuccessful, they make adjustments until they find a successful method.

- **Negative reinforcement** — saying nothing when a *correct* action is shown, after a period of criticism about a performance.
- **Punishment** — strategy used to reduce or eliminate undesirable actions.

Social learning: observational learning (Bandura)

- Learn by watching and copying significant others.
- Most likely to copy model if they share characteristics such as age/gender.
- Likely to copy successful actions and those that have been reinforced.

Bandura's model

Attention:

- Coach ensures that the performer *concentrates* on the model.
- Coach *points out* key cues in the demonstration.

Retention:

- Coach ensures the performer *remembers* the demonstration/mental image.
- Demonstration should be *repeated*.

Motor reproduction:

- Performer must be *physically and mentally able* to copy the model demonstration.

Motivation:

- Performer must have the *drive* to copy and learn the skill
- Offer *praise* or *rewards*.

Constructivism: social development theory (Vygotsky)

Social interaction plays a key role in an individual's development.

Role of social interaction

- **Inter-psychological learning** — happens before development. A performer learns from people with whom they interact.
- **Intra-psychological learning** — the individual thinks about what they can do on their own and what they have learned from others.
- **More knowledgeable other (MKO)** — a person who has a greater understanding of the task than you do. They offer technical advice and feedback.
- **Zone of proximal development** — what the learner can do when the MKO helps.
  - **Stage 1** — what the performer can achieve independently.
  - **Stage 2** — what the performer can achieve with help from the MKO.
  - **Stage 3** — what the performer cannot do at this moment in time.

> **Exam tip**
>
> A common mistake is to confuse negative reinforcement with negative feedback. Negative reinforcement is a way of ensuring that a correct response is repeated (by saying nothing negative), whereas negative feedback informs the performer of incorrect actions.

> **Exam tip**
>
> Students often find this section tricky and give vague/generalised answers. Ensure that you use the correct terminology for each theory to access the marks.

> **Knowledge check 23**
>
> What are the four main parts of Bandura's model?

> **Knowledge check 24**
>
> Describe the zone of proximal development.

Summary

After studying this topic you should be able to:

- describe the characteristics of each stage of learning and give examples to illustrate performers' movements in each stage
- draw, label and describe the learning curve
- explain the causes of, and give solutions for, a plateau in learning
- explain the key aspects of each of the four theories of learning
- describe how skills are learned as suggested by each theory and give practical examples to illustrate them

Use of guidance and feedback

Methods of guidance

Verbal guidance

Verbal guidance is giving the performer instructions on what to do and how to do it, for example explaining that the front crawl leg kick should come from the hip and not the knee. It is useful for autonomous performers and can be used to give tactical, strategic or technical information.

Advantages

- It can be given immediately.
- It is very useful for open skills.
- It can be used effectively in conjunction with visual guidance.

Disadvantages

- There is a chance of information overload if too many instructions are given together, and the performer may lose concentration.
- Cognitive performers may not understand the technical terms used by their coach.

Visual guidance

Visual guidance allows the performer to see how to perform the skill. It is essential for cognitive performers. Examples include demonstrations, coaching manuals and charts, for example the coach shows a video of how to perform a tumble turn in swimming.

Advantages

- It shows the performer exactly what the skill should look like.
- It builds a clear mental image.
- Highlights weaknesses.

Disadvantages

- It can cause information overload.
- The demonstration must be accurate, or an incorrect movement pattern will be copied.

Manual and mechanical guidance

Manual guidance is the use of physical support or when a coach forces a response from the performer, for example holding a beginner swimmer up in the water to keep them afloat.

Mechanical guidance involves using equipment to aid and shape movement, for example using a swimming float/armband for safety.

Advantages

- They are effective for cognitive performers.
- They can be used for dangerous tasks because they improve safety during performance, while also reducing fear/anxiety.
- The performer can build their confidence.
- Because the whole skill can be attempted, kinaesthesis can also be developed.

> **Knowledge check 25**
>
> What are the advantages of manual and mechanical guidance?

Disadvantages

- The performer may become reliant on them and may also become demotivated.
- Incorrect kinaesthesis can be produced and as a result bad habits might form.
- When using manual guidance, the physical contact or proximity of the coach can make the performer feel uncomfortable and/or could be misconstrued.

Purposes and types of feedback

There are several types of feedback used in sport. It is essential to enable players to improve their performance. Feedback is information given to performers to reinforce and refine their actions. Table 10 describes the types of feedback and how they are used.

Table 10 Feedback in sport

Type of feedback	Description and uses
Knowledge of performance (KP)	Information about *why* the skill/action was successful/unsuccessful, including technical information
Knowledge of results (KR)	Information about whether or not the skill/action was successful
Positive	Information about what was *correct*, so that it will be repeated in the future
Negative	Information about *incorrect actions*, so that errors are corrected
Intrinsic	From *within* using *kinaesthesis* Used to 'feel' if the action was correct or not Can be positive or negative
Extrinsic	From an *outside* source Used to reinforce correct actions and correct errors Can be positive or negative

Exam tip

Students find guidance and feedback easy to learn but often miss marks because they fail to give practical examples. Remember that sometimes no example means no marks, even if your description is correct.

Knowledge check 26

What is the difference between knowledge of results and knowledge of performance?

Summary

After studying this topic you should be able to:
- explain each of the four types of guidance and explain the impact that each type will have on the development of skills
- explain each of the six types of feedback and explain the impact that each type will have on the development of skills
- give practical examples to illustrate your answers

Exam tip

This section is theory heavy and you will be asked to apply your knowledge to sporting situations. Ensure that you use correct terminology.

Memory models

General information processing model

Information processing describes how performers receive information from the sporting environment, rationalise the information and decide what to do with it before finally initiating a response, i.e. performing the action.

- **Input** — senses (eyes — vision, ears — audition, proprioceptors — touch, balance and kinaesthesis) gather cues from the display. Perception, through the DCR process, is used to make judgements about and filter the environmental cues as relevant or irrelevant by selective attention. The performer focuses on the relevant stimuli and ignores the irrelevant noise.

Knowledge check 27

Describe the input phase of information processing.

- **Decision making** — a decision on what course of action to take is made. The memory system is engaged and previous experiences are reflected on. The relevant motor programme is retrieved and sent to the muscles in readiness to produce the action.
- **Output** — the skill is produced.
- **Feedback** — the performer receives information about the action that they have produced during and after the performance.

The working memory model

This model has a supervisory system called the **central executive** and three 'slave' systems (Figure 12). The central executive maintains overall control. It links with the long-term memory, focuses and switches attention if required, but has limited capacity. It identifies which information goes to which subsystem, as these perform different functions.

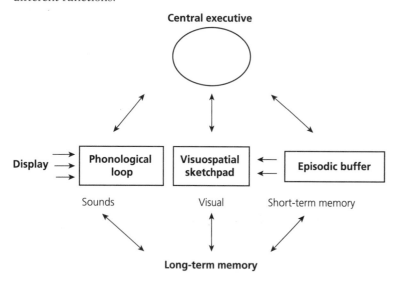

Figure 12 The Baddeley and Hitch working memory model

- The **phonological loop** deals with auditory information, for example it processes the call from your team mate. It is a temporary storage system, which creates a memory trace that is sent to the long-term memory to trigger the motor programme. The memory trace will fade away if it is not rehearsed, for example you might repeatedly say out loud the moves in your trampoline ten-bounce routine so that you do not forget the order.
- The **visuospatial sketchpad** holds visual and spatial information temporarily, for example images of set plays and where you would be during the action. It also stores kinaesthetic information about how the movement feels.
- The **episodic buffer** stores three/four chunks or 'episodes'. It allows different parts of the working memory system to talk to each other and produces sequences of information to send to the long-term memory, which initiates the motor programme. It also gathers perceptual information, for example information about the flight of the ball as you receive a cross, the sound of the 'man on!' call from the coach, and also how the limbs and muscles feel as you move to receive the ball.

The **phonological loop** is a temporary storage system that deals with auditory information. It creates a memory trace and triggers the motor programme.

Knowledge check 28

Describe the visuospatial sketchpad.

Functions and characteristics of the working memory and long-term memory

■ The working memory receives the relevant information that has been filtered away from the irrelevant by selective attention.

■ It has a limited capacity; it can store 7 ± 2 items for up to approximately 30 seconds.

■ If a skill is practised/rehearsed, it can be transferred to the long-term memory and stored as a motor programme.

■ The working memory produces a memory trace if the current skill is compared to information stored in the long-term memory.

■ The long-term memory then sends the motor programme to the working memory to use in the current sporting situation.

■ The long-term memory has an unlimited capacity and stores information for an unlimited time.

■ Once the long-term memory sends the motor programme to the working memory, it initiates the motor programme.

Strategies to increase the retention and retrieval of information

■ **Practice/rehearsal** — to groove the skill. This will help to create the motor programmes that are stored in the long-term memory.

■ **Linking/association with past experiences** — relating the new information to that already stored.

■ **Chunking** — small groups of information are put together and memorised as one.

■ **Enjoyable/fun experiences** — positive experiences are readily remembered.

■ **Meaningful** — the learner should understand the relevance of the information to them and their performance.

■ **Chaining** — information should be presented in an organised, sequential manner to make it easy to remember.

■ **Mental rehearsal/imagery** — visualising the skill or going over it in your mind.

■ **Reinforcement** — if learners receive positive feedback or reinforcement, or are rewarded with praise after a correct response, they are more likely to remember the information.

> **Exam tip**
>
> Remember that characteristics make up a description or the features of the system, whereas functions relate to the job it does. Questions could ask about either or both.

> **Chunking** involves grouping information together and memorising it all as one to increase the capacity of the memory.

Summary

After studying this topic you should be able to:

■ describe the four main stages of information processing and give practical examples to support your answers

■ describe the functions and characteristics of Baddeley and Hitch's working memory model

■ describe strategies for increasing memory retention and retrieval of information

■ give strategies to improve information processing

Efficiency of information processing

Whiting's model

Whiting's model illustrates how information is processed in more detail (Figure 13). The key features and functions are described below.

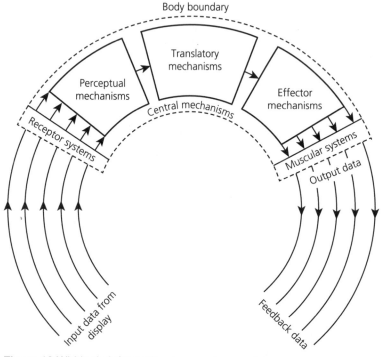

Figure 13 Whiting's information-processing model

Environment

Contains all the information required to perform the skill/action.

Display

This is the sporting environment and all the information contained in it, for example when serving in tennis this includes the ball, racquet, court, umpire, line judges, crowd and opponent.

Sensory organs/receptor systems

- Vision, for example seeing the ball and opponents.
- Audition, for example hearing the shouts from your coach.
- Proprioception — information about the position of your body, including:
  - **touch**, for example the feeling of equipment on the skin
  - **kinaesthesis** — the internal muscle feelings
  - **equilibrium** — information about whether the body is balanced

Exam tip

Questions will ask you to apply Whiting's model to a practical situation. Ensure that you name a skill rather than simply stating 'the skill'.

Perceptual mechanisms

A **judgement** is made regarding the incoming information received by the sense organs. Perception includes the **DCR process**.

Selective attention occurs, which means that the relevant information, such as the ball, opponents and team mates, is focused on, whereas the irrelevant information, for example the crowd and linesman, is filtered away. Only the relevant information is acted upon while the irrelevant information is disregarded.

Selective attention is important because it:

- aids concentration
- improves reaction time
- filters out any distractions
- controls arousal levels
- reduces the chance of information overload in the short-term memory, for example focusing on the ball, service box and opponent's position.

Translatory mechanisms

A decision is made on what action should be taken, with the help of previous experiences stored in the memory. A **motor programme** is selected, for example choosing a fast, wide serve because your opponent has been unable to return these before.

Effector mechanisms

Once the motor programme is selected, impulses are sent to the working muscles to carry out the movement, for example sending motor programme information to deltoids, biceps, triceps etc. via nervous impulses.

Muscular systems

The muscles that are needed to produce the action receive these impulses and are ready to move, for example the deltoids, biceps, triceps etc. receive the information and prepare to serve.

Output data

The movement/action is performed — the fast, wide serve is completed.

Feedback data

Information about the effectiveness of the movement is received. This can be intrinsic/extrinsic/positive/negative, for example as you produce the serve your kinaesthetic awareness tells you that you have overhit the serve. The umpire also calls the serve out.

The **DCR process** refers to detection (receiving cues), comparison (cues compared with memories) and recognition (understanding what response is required).

Selective attention involves focusing on the relevant environmental information and disregarding irrelevant information.

Knowledge check 29

What is the function of the effector mechanism?

Reaction time and anticipation

Table 11 shows some key definitions of reaction times and anticipation.

Table 11 Key definitions of reaction times and anticipation

Simple reaction time	One stimulus and one response. For example, in a swimming race, the stimulus is the starter signal and the only appropriate response is to dive in.
Choice reaction time	Several stimuli and several possible responses. For example, in football in open play, you may have several team mates calling for a pass and several possible responses in terms of who you pass to, type of pass etc.
Reaction time	Time from the stimulus being presented to the performer beginning to respond to it. It is the time from the onset of the stimulus to the onset of the response.
Movement time	Time from the beginning of the action to the end of the action. It is the time from the onset of the action to the completion of the task.
Response time	Reaction time plus movement time. It is the time from the onset of the stimulus to the completion of the task.
Anticipation	Predicting that a stimulus will be presented before it happens.
Temporal anticipation	Predicting when the stimulus will be presented.
Spatial anticipation	Predicting where and what is going to happen.

Factors affecting response time

Hick's law

Hick's law describes the impact of choice reaction time on performance (Figure 14). It suggests that as the number of choices increases, so does the time it takes to react, in other words the more choices there are, the slower the reaction time. However, this theory suggests that reaction time does not increase proportionately with the number of choices — moving from one to two or three choices results in a dramatic increase in reaction time, but with several responses reaction time is not affected as severely. A lower response rate is experienced with increasing number of choices. Understanding this theory can help you to slow down your opponents' responses by presenting them with a range of options during play.

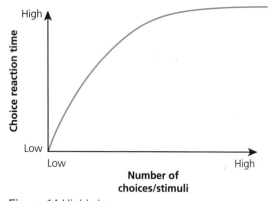

Figure 14 Hick's law

What is the difference between temporal and spatial anticipation?

Exam tip

Do not use the word 'react' in your answers about reaction time.

Exam tip

If reaction time increases, the performance is getting worse not better.

Single channel hypothesis

The single channel hypothesis suggests that we can detect many stimuli at once, but we can only *process* one piece of information at a time (Figure 15). Any further stimuli that are presented must wait to be processed, even if the performer recognises that the second stimulus is actually the correct piece of information. This causes a 'bottleneck' to occur. Just as Hick's law states, the more stimuli presented, the slower the reaction time.

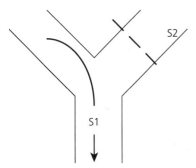

Figure 15 The single channel hypothesis: only one stimulus can be processed at a time

Psychological refractory period

Although the single channel hypothesis explains that we can only process one stimulus at once, often performers are presented with multiple stimuli at a time. If multiple stimuli are presented, this can cause a delay in processing — the performer may physically freeze. This delay is known as the psychological refractory period (Figure 16). This is caused by a second stimulus arriving before the first has been processed. It can be used by performers to slow their opposition down by increasing their reaction time.

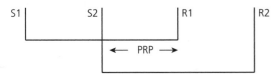

Figure 16 The psychological refractory period

An example is disguising a drop shot in badminton:

■ First stimulus (S1): the player sets their body position as if to play an overhead clear to the back of the court.
■ First response (R1): the opponent anticipates the overhead clear and begins to travel towards the back of the court to return the shot.
■ Second stimulus (S2): the player actually plays a drop shot, not an overhead clear.
■ Second response (R2) the opponent changes direction and attempts to respond to the actual drop shot rather than the anticipated overhead clear.

Exam tip

Do not use abbreviations such as PRP. Write the full technical term in your answers.

Exam tip

Each of the above theories has a diagram associated with it. If it does not form part of the question, you should draw it and use it to help you focus your answer. Do not forget to label it fully.

Knowledge check 31

What causes the psychological refractory period?

Strategies to improve response time

- **Practice** — the more you respond to a stimulus, the faster your reactions become.
- **Selective attention** — focus and concentrate on only the relevant information.
- **Mental rehearsal** — go over the performance in your mind.
- **Improve fitness levels** — the fitter you are, the quicker you can respond.
- **Warm up** — if the body and mind are prepared, you can respond more quickly.
- **Gain optimum arousal** — if you are at the peak of your arousal, you will respond more quickly.
- **Detect cues early** — analyse your opponent's play, for example body/limb positions and line out calls, in order to anticipate what they intend to do next.
- **Anticipation** — predict that a movement will happen before it occurs.

The **recall schema** stores information about the movement and initiates the movement.

The **recognition schema** controls and evaluates the movement.

Schmidt's schema theory

A schema is a generalised motor programme that is made up of two components — **recall schema** and **recognition schema**. Table 12 shows the two components of a schema and the four memory items. The example included illustrates how a footballer selects and initiates a pass, before completing and evaluating the action.

Table 12 Schema theory

Recall schema: 1 Stores information about the movement 2 Initiates the movement		Recognition schema: 3 Controls the movement 4 Evaluates the movement	
1 Initial conditions	2 Response specification	3 Sensory consequences	4 Response outcome
Information is gathered about whether you have been here or somewhere similar before. Information about the environment and your body is collated.	(Based on the initial conditions) you decide what movement to perform.	Information is gathered about the movement using intrinsic feedback or kinaesthesis.	Information is gathered concerning the result of the movement. Was it successful or unsuccessful?
Example: I play on the left wing in football. I have the ball at my feet and I have made a run down the wing and am curving toward the area. Our centre forward is making a run towards the goal on my right and the keeper has come off his line and is attempting to close me down. I remember being in similar situations in training and previous games.	Example: I think about chipping the keeper but instead decide to send a lofted pass on to the head of the centre forward who has made the run. The pass is high, mid pace and slightly in front of him.	Example: As I pass the football, I feel the ball leave my foot with the correct amount of power and weight to reach the centre forward.	Example: The pass was timed perfectly. The centre forward connected with the ball and scored the goal.

To develop schemata:

- Use **varied practice** to build a range of experience.
- Ensure practised skills are **transferable** from training to the game situation.
- Give a range of **feedback** regularly.
- Give **praise** and positive reinforcement.
- **Practise** a range of skills until they are grooved.

Exam tip

You will be asked to apply Schmidt's schema theory to practical situations. Ensure that you keep the same example throughout and explain the sections in order.

Knowledge check 32

Describe sensory consequences.

Summary

After studying this topic you should be able to:

- describe each component of Whiting's model and apply sporting examples to each part
- define reaction time, movement time and response time, and understand the relationship between them
- describe simple and choice reaction time, and give practical examples to support your answer
- describe the factors affecting response time as suggested by Hick's law, the single channel hypothesis and the psychological refractory period
- define temporal and spatial anticipation, and give practical examples to support your answer
- give strategies to improve response time
- explain Schmidt's schema theory and apply each component to sporting situations

■ Sport and society

Emergence of globalisation of sport in the twenty-first century

Characteristics of popular recreation in pre-industrial Britain (pre-1780)

Mob football

Mob football is an example of an activity played by the lower classes in pre-industrial Britain, which reflected the characteristics of popular recreation and sociocultural factors evident at the time (Table 13). It was also an example of the clear division of such a **feudal society** into two tiers, with certain sports for the lower classes to participate in (e.g. mob football) and other sports that involved the upper class (e.g. real tennis).

Table 13 The link between sociocultural features in pre-industrial Britain and popular recreation activities of the time for the lower class

Sociocultural features/characteristics of pre-industrial Britain (i.e. for the lower class pre-1780)	Popular recreation features/characteristics to reflect this in the lower class (e.g. mob football)
Limited transport/communications for the lower class	Local — sport was localised/restricted to the areas and played in the communities where people lived
Illiteracy common in the uneducated lower class	Simple/basic rules/lack of codification/limited organisation/locally set rules (e.g. no set space)
Harsh society/life was cruel for the lower class	Violent — sport was violent/aggressive/unruly in nature and male dominated, with wagering/gambling on the outcome
Seasonal time/work linked to the agricultural calendar/very long working hours for the lower class in 'cottage-based industries' (i.e. paid in kind)	Occasional — mob football was only played occasionally/annually/as part of a festival occasion (e.g. holy days)
Pre-industrial revolution/pre-urbanisation — the majority of the lower-class population lived in the countryside/small villages in an agriculturally based society (i.e. agrarian)	Rural/natural — mob football was played in the countryside/rural areas, where people lived, using the natural resources they had available (e.g. a pig's bladder as a ball)
Two-tier class system/feudal system (there was no middle class at this stage)	Class divisions — there was a clear division/separation between activities played by the lower class (e.g. mob games) and upper class (e.g. real tennis), i.e. class was a key influence on the activities undertaken in pre-industrial Britain

Real tennis

Real tennis (also called 'royal tennis'/'the sport of kings') was another sport played in pre-industrial Britain. As a feature of upper-class life, it did not reflect the typical popular recreation characteristics of many activities at the time and was more typical of **rational recreation** (i.e. a more structured/organised/civilised activity).

■ It was an exclusive activity, courtly and royal in nature, played by the upper-class males of the two-tier society evident at the time (e.g. by Henry VIII, who had a real tennis court at Hampton Court).

■ The upper classes were educated and highly literate, so complex rules could be written down for the sport and could be readily understood and applied (i.e. it was codified).

Exam tip

Exam questions on popular recreation will require you to illustrate your understanding of class as a key defining feature of participation in sport in pre-industrial Britain (i.e. pre-1780).

A **feudal society** is structured around a relationship derived from the holding of land in exchange for services or labour.

Rational recreation was participation in sport that was characterised by features such as respectability, regularity and rules.

Knowledge check 33

Identify the characteristics of popular recreation in pre-industrial Britain.

- The upper class played real tennis to a high moral code, so it lacked violence and was instead played in a civilised manner, with mutual respect, reflecting the participants' society.
- With plenty of leisure time, the upper class were able to play real tennis on a regular basis, developing their skills/techniques to a high level in many cases.
- Using their wealth, the upper class played real tennis in expensive, purpose-built facilities, using specialist equipment (e.g. racquets).
- The upper class also had the ability to travel to play real tennis, so it was non-local in nature.
- Wagering (i.e. betting) was common on the outcome of matches.

Table 14 compares the sports of mob football and real tennis.

Table 14 Comparison of the characteristics of mob football for the lower class with real tennis for the upper class

Characteristics	Mob football	Real tennis
Participation	Played by the lower classes	Played by the upper classes/courtly in nature
Rules	Few/simple/locally agreed	Complex/written
Conduct	Violent/unruly	Non-violent/civilised
Frequency of play	Occasional/annual/linked to festival occasions	Regularly played; highly skilled performance evident
Facilities/equipment	Played in the natural environment, using the natural resources available	Played in purpose-built facilities, using specialist equipment

Knowledge check 34

Explain the characteristics of real tennis in pre-industrial Britain.

Exam tip

Questions may require you to make a direct comparison between lower- and upper-class sporting participation in pre-industrial Britain. Make one direct comparison at a time, based on the main characteristics identified in Table 14 (e.g. participation, rules).

Summary

After studying this topic you should be able to:
- identify and explain the characteristics of pre-industrial society and their impact on sporting recreation at the time
- identify and explain the characteristics of popular recreation for the lower class (e.g. mob football) and rational recreation for the upper class (e.g. real tennis)

Industrial and post-industrial development of sport (1780–1900)

This section of the specification involves the study of sociocultural factors and how they influenced the development of structured, organised sport (i.e. rational recreation) for the masses in the late eighteenth/nineteenth centuries. Links will be made, as appropriate, to the development of association football, lawn tennis and track-and-field athletics as newly rationalised activities during this period.

The Industrial Revolution and provision through factories

The influence of the **Industrial Revolution** on the development of rationalised sports and pastimes changed during the nineteenth century. In the first half, the initial effects were often negative, as outlined below:

- **Poor health and hygiene** — poor working and living conditions led to pollution and a lack of hygiene, with associated illness, which meant less energy for playing sport.
- **Lack of income** — low wages and poverty were evident, with little spare income for leisure pursuits.
- **Lack of leisure time** — a shift from 'seasonal time' to 'machine time', leading to long, 12-hour working days, 6 days a week; the Sabbath (i.e. Sunday) was for religious observance.
- **Lack of facility provision** — no working-class access to sports facilities.
- **Overcrowding and lack of space** — migration of the lower classes into urban areas, to look for work in the new factories being built, led to overcrowding and a loss of space in which to play traditional mob games.
- **Loss of rights** — restrictions were placed on mob games through changes in criminal laws.

In the second half of the nineteenth century, improvements had a positive effect, as outlined below:

- Health and hygiene improved as a result of gradual improvements in living and working conditions (e.g. local council provision of public baths to improve cleanliness), enabling more energy/willingness for sport.
- There was a gradual increase in wages and more time for sport due to the Factory Acts, with Saturday half-days being implemented for the workers (i.e. a decrease in working hours).
- The emergence of the new middle class changed behaviour and ways of playing. Sport became more acceptable and respectable, and was played to a high moral code. The middle class developed strict rules, leagues and competitions; they provided facilities/public parks via their involvement in the local council; they offered more time off work and broken time payments etc.
- Industrial patronage (i.e. kind factory owners becoming 'patrons of sport' for the working class by providing opportunities for them to participate in various ways) led to provision for recreation and sport. Factory teams were set up and sporting facilities were provided.
- New inventions, for example manufactured sports equipment such as goal posts and goal nets, as well as clothing/kits, could now be manufactured in industrial mills.

Urbanisation

The following is a summary of the key features of **urbanisation** that contributed to the development of sport in this period:

- **Lack of space** — space was at a premium in cities. This led to the development of purpose-built facilities to play sport (e.g. football grounds).

The **Industrial Revolution** is deemed to have occurred between the mid-eighteenth and mid-nineteenth centuries. This period marked a change in Britain from a feudal, rural society into an industrialised, machine-based, capitalist society, controlled by a powerful urban middle class.

Exam tip

You can remember the initial negative effects of industrialisation using the acronym **HIT FOR**:

H = poor **h**ealth and **h**ygiene
I = lack of **i**ncome
T = lack of leisure **t**ime
F = lack of **f**acility provision
O = **o**vercrowding and lack of space
R = loss of **r**ights

Urbanisation involved large numbers of people migrating/moving from rural areas into towns and cities, to seek regular work in the factories.

Knowledge check 35

Explain the impact of urbanisation on the development of sport during the nineteenth century.

- **Large working-class populations** — urbanisation meant a large working-class population that needed entertaining, resulting in mass spectator numbers at football matches for the first time.
- **Loss of traditional sports** — many traditional working-class sports, such as mob games, were banned in a civilised urban society, so there was a need for new sports to emerge.

Transport and communication

The development of the railways contributed to the development of sport:

- **Movement of teams/spectators** — the development of the railways/steam trains enabled faster and further travel for players and fans alike, leading to the development of nationwide fixtures.
- **Improved access to different parts of the country** — nationwide train travel enabled sport to develop from local to regional to national, with a need for a single set of rules to develop and the formation of leagues involving clubs from across the country (e.g. the Football League, 1888).
- **Cheaper train travel** — rail travel became relatively cheap/affordable with the introduction of third-class tickets, allowing the working class to follow their teams at home and away.

In terms of 'communications', industrial Britain underwent a gradual improvement in educational provision:

- Rules could be developed further and more people could understand them.
- Developments in the printed media increased knowledge and awareness of sport in a number of ways (e.g. fixture dates and results of matches). This led to the emergence of sporting heroes/role models because people could read match reports and relate to their favourite players.

The British Empire

Sport was seen as a powerful way of instilling moral values into people across the world and of binding the various people of the Empire together. Young men educated to become leaders of the British Empire spread the playing of games in a variety of ways:

- As **teachers** they developed teams and taught traditional sporting values in schools throughout the Empire.
- As **industrialists/factory owners** they set up teams and gave workers time off to play competitive sport nationally and internationally.
- As **clergy** they developed church teams/became missionaries and took sport abroad (good for social control/morality etc.).
- As **officers in the British army** they used sport with the armed services and spread sport throughout the Empire.
- As **diplomats** they travelled the world and took sport with them (e.g. rugby).
- They formed the national governing bodies of sport (e.g. the RFU), which codified sports and established leagues and competitions that spread internationally as well as nationally.

> **Exam tip**
>
> The characteristics of urbanisation and its impact on the development of sport can be remembered using the three Ls:
>
> - Lack of space
> - Large working-class population
> - Loss of traditional sports

The Church

The reasons why the Church promoted sport are as follows:

- Sport encouraged social control (i.e. improved behaviour) through 'civilised' activities that diverted people away from less socially acceptable activities, such as drinking. Church facilities, such as halls, provided venues for 'improving the morality' of the working classes by 'Muscular Christians'. Former public schoolboys promoted this **Muscular Christianity** by engaging the community and attempting to eradicate the excesses of working-class behavior, such as drinking, in favour of more healthy pursuits.
- Sport was viewed as a good way of promoting Christian values. The development of the YMCA promoted the healthy body/healthy mind link. The clergy viewed sport as a good way to increase church attendance.

The following points explain how churches helped provide more opportunities for sporting involvement:

- The approval/active involvement of the clergy encouraged the working classes to participate in rationalised sporting activities, for example association football.
- Churches set up clubs, for example Aston Villa was established by Villa Cross Methodist Church.
- They provided facilities for playing sport (e.g. church halls).
- They formed church groups, with sporting involvement a key part of their programmes of activities, for example the YMCA.

Local authorities

The development of **public provision** (e.g. baths in urban and industrial areas) positively influenced the opportunities for working-class, rational recreation. To try to improve the health and hygiene of the working classes, local authorities felt a civic responsibility to apply for grants to provide public washing facilities and improve their status as a town (e.g. via the Baths and Washhouses Act of 1846). Increased provision was made in the second half of the nineteenth century for public bath houses, with first- and second-class facilities to reflect the social class divisions. Plunge baths developed for swimming/recreational use.

Three-tier class system and the emergence of the middle class (e.g. as factory owners)

The following is a summary of the key ways in which members of the middle class supported developments in sport:

- **Codification** — the development of strict rules as public school/university old boys played a key role in the formation of many national governing bodies (NGBs) of sport. They controlled sport and became key organisers via their administration experience, which enabled them to form and run clubs and NGBs, for example the FA was established in 1863.
- **Competitions** — the development of leagues and competitions via middle-class involvement in NGBs/factory teams.
- **Public provision** — the development of public facilities (e.g. parks and public baths) via middle-class **philanthropists** and the passing of government Acts in their roles as local politicians.

Muscular Christianity was a movement that emerged in mid-nineteenth-century England that was characterised by a belief in manliness, the moral and physical beauty of athleticism, teamwork, discipline and self-sacrifice.

Knowledge check 36

Describe how the Church encouraged the post-industrial rational game of football.

Public provision involved local council provision of facilities (e.g. parks and baths) for the masses to participate in physical activity.

Philanthropists were kind, generous, middle-class individuals who had a social conscience and were keen to try to provide for a better life among the working class.

- **Increased leisure time** — middle-class factory owners gradually gave their workers more leisure time (e.g. a Saturday half day), which allowed more time to watch/participate in sport.
- **Move to 'professionalism'** — the middle class helped in the development of early commercial/professional sport, for example acting as agents and promoters in athletics or as factory owners setting up factory teams.

Development of national governing bodies

The factors that led to the emergence of national governing bodies of sport during the nineteenth century were as follows:

- **Clubs** — lots more people were playing sports (e.g. football), leading to more clubs forming, which required an organisation for them to join/affiliate to.
- **Control** — there was a need for an organisation to have overall control of the development of a sport as more clubs formed. This included 'control of eligibility', i.e. who could play their sport and who could not. For example, Rugby Union had an exclusion clause (i.e. manual labour clause), which meant that only amateurs could play it, effectively keeping the working classes out.
- **Codification** — NGBs were required to develop rules into one recognised system or code, i.e. codification via standard rules for playing a sport.
- **Competitions** — more clubs forming led to an increased demand for regular fixtures/ leagues/cup competitions, for example the Football League was founded 1888.

Exam tip

Think about the four Cs when referring to the emergence of national governing bodies of sport during the nineteenth century:
- **C**lubs
- **C**ontrol
- **C**odification
- **C**ompetitions

'Rationalised' sport

Lawn tennis

The characteristics of rational recreation/sport evident in lawn tennis include the following:

- Highly structured/codified, with set rules, for example the court size/scoring system.
- Institutionalised/has a national governing body, for example the LTA.
- Has officials, for example line judges.
- Players play for extrinsic rewards, for example high levels of prize money.
- Highly skilled/involves strategies and tactics, for example shot variation used to outwit an opponent.

The following is a summary of the key features of lawn tennis as it developed in the industrial/post-industrial era:

- **Middle-class invention** — it developed as an affordable alternative to real tennis, which set the middle class apart from the working class and led to private clubs developing for participation.
- **Played by the middle class** — it was played in middle-class gardens on lawns big enough to house private tennis courts.
- **Organised by the middle class** — the middle class had the organisational experience necessary to form their own private clubs.

- **Use of specialist equipment** — the middle class had sufficient funds to purchase their own equipment.
- **Use of standardised rules** — Wingfield's 'kit' contained a rulebook that helped standardise the game, with lawn tennis played to the same rules no matter where it was played.
- **Played by males and females** — tennis was a good 'social game' that both sexes could play.

Track-and-field athletics

The industrialisation of society led to rural fairs being replaced by urban fairs, as people migrated in large numbers to towns and cities to look for work. Athletics events became popular in such areas, with purpose-built tracks and facilities found in most major cities by the mid-nineteenth century.

Walking and running races took place over set distances on race courses. Large numbers of people attended athletics events, with up to 25,000 spectators at meetings as the nineteenth century progressed. Class divisions were evident as it became a 'rationalised' activity. Upper- and middle-class amateurs ran for enjoyment or to test themselves, whereas the lower classes ran to make money and were deemed 'professionals'.

The role of the Wenlock Olympian Games

By 1867 the programme for the Wenlock Olympian Games featured a range of early athletics events, many of which were later developed into track-and-field events. Examples included: under-14 boys 100 yards, a mile foot race, running high leap/long leap, putting the stone and hammer throwing.

Association football

A variety of reasons can be given to explain the growth and development of association football from the mid-nineteenth century:

- **Urbanisation** — large numbers of people living in one place provided a large captive audience for football. The lack of space in urban areas led to purpose-built, specialist facilities for playing football, with terraces to satisfy the high spectator demand.
- **More free time/increased leisure time** — as workers spent less time in the factories, more time was available to them for watching/playing sport (e.g. Saturday at 3 p.m.).
- **More disposable income** — improved standards of living as a result of higher wages gave the working class enough money to pay entrance fees.
- **Improved transport** — the development of the train network enabled fans to travel to watch away fixtures.
- **Increased professionalism** — the opportunities to play football professionally gradually increased, for example through broken-time payments.
- **Increased organisation** — football quickly became highly structured and standardised. National rules and codification meant the game was far less violent, which reflected an increasingly civilised society.

Exam tip

The aims of Wenlock Olympian Games can be remembered using the acronym **LIMP**:
L = lower class participation
I = intellectual improvement
M = moral improvement
P = physical improvement

Knowledge check 37

Explain how association football in the nineteenth century reflected the characteristics of sport.

The changing role of women in sport

During the post-industrial era women's participation in sport was affected by a number of negative myths/restrictions, which gradually reduced over time. These included:

- the traditional viewpoint that sport was a 'male preserve'
- sport being viewed as 'too aggressive'/'too competitive' for women and leading to 'over exertion'
- the belief in the early twentieth century that sports participation had a negative impact on fertility/child-bearing capacity
- clothing requirements for women (e.g. corsets and long dresses), which restricted their participation

The exception to the rule was lawn tennis, which was viewed as an important activity in the emancipation of women and was accepted as a game middle-class women could play towards the end of the nineteenth century for the following reasons:

- It could be played in the privacy of gardens, behind hedges, thus protecting their modesty.
- It was played as part of social gatherings of both sexes.
- It could be played without over-exertion/aggression, as a 'minimum-exercise activity', but with health benefits.
- It could be played despite the restrictive clothing rules of the time (e.g. long dresses).
- Positive female role models of the time encouraged participation (e.g. Lottie Dod).

Knowledge check 38

Identify the reasons why women's participation in sport was restricted in the nineteenth century.

The status of amateur and professional performers

Table 15 Characteristics of amateur and professional performers

Characteristics	Gentleman amateur	Working-class professional
Time	Part of leisured class (upper class did not have to work) — regular participation	Very little free time to participate; working class had to hold down a job alongside playing sport
Ethics/morality	Played sport to a high moral code (e.g. sportsmanship)	Played sport to low levels of morality (viewed as corruptible)
Number of sports	Played lots of sports, using natural talents — the all-rounder was 'revered'	Specialised in a single sport and trained hard to improve
Status/wealth	High status in society; wealthy (public school background) — could play sport 'for the love of it'	Low status; limited wealth (state school background) — needed 'financial compensation' to play sport

Summary

After studying this topic you should be able to:

- identify and explain the characteristics and impact on sport (i.e. rationalised football, lawn tennis and athletics) of a range of sociocultural factors, including the Industrial Revolution, urbanisation, transport and communications, the British Empire, the Church, local authorities, the emergence of the middle classes, and national governing bodies
- consider the changing role of women in sport as the nineteenth century progressed
- identify the characteristics of amateur and professional performers in the nineteenth century, and how these impacted on their sporting involvement

Exam tip

You can remember the characteristics of amateur and professional performers, and the impact of these on sporting participation in the post-industrial era, using the acronym **TENS**:

T = time
E = ethics/morality
N = number of sports
S = status/wealth

Post World War 2 (1950 to present)

Characteristics and impact on sport of the golden triangle

Sport, the media and business/**sponsorship** are all strongly interlinked and mutually dependent; this is known as the 'golden triangle'. Each element of the 'triangle' relies on the others. For example, without media coverage, sports are less attractive to sponsors who want their business or product to be publicised to as many people as possible. The media use sport to gain viewers, listeners and readers. In turn, businesses and sponsors use the media to advertise their products and services.

Benefits of sponsorship for sports performers
- Increased wages and prize money.
- Increased availability of professional contracts. Performers are able to devote themselves full time to sport, training harder and longer to improve performance.
- Performers are increasingly in the public eye and well known, so they need to maintain discipline and behave appropriately to project a positive image (e.g. on-field via fair play; off-field via community/charitable work).
- Increased funding pays for access to high-quality training support and specialist equipment etc.

Benefits of sponsorship to companies of investing large amounts of money in sport
- Increased publicity/advertising, leading to increased sales of a product and thus increased profit to the company.
- Creates a positive association between a brand/product and a healthy sporting image, for example an elite athlete (e.g. Quorn and Mo Farah).
- A decrease in tax paid by a company due to tax relief on money 'donated' as sponsorship.
- Companies can use sport as a means of corporate hospitality, for example by entertaining clients/potential clients at major sporting events.

Commercial sport, as evident in association football, tennis and athletics, involves:
- **professional sport** — it is high quality
- **sponsorship and business** — these go hand-in-hand
- **entertainment** — watching sport is part of a mass-entertainment industry; viewing needs to fit into a relatively short time scale
- **contracts** — for example, selling of merchandise and bidding for television rights
- **athletes as commodities** — for example, as an asset to companies through product endorsement, which increases sales/profits
- **a wide level of media coverage** — interest in high-profile sports with visual appeal, high skill levels, well-matched competition and simple rules

There are a number of different types of **media** involved in covering sport, such as newspapers, radio, the internet and social media. TV can be viewed as the most powerful aspect of the media — it is now global, so the buying and selling of TV broadcasting rights is a very important part of twenty-first-century sport.

Sponsorship is when a company pays sporting events or performers to advertise its products in return for an increase in sales of its products.

Exam tip

If a question uses 'explain', make sure that your answers are detailed and linked together using words such as 'via', 'due to' and 'because'.

Knowledge check 39

Identify the characteristics of a sport that make it attractive for TV coverage.

A number of changes in media coverage of sport from the late twentieth century onwards can be identified:

■ Coverage via lots of different types of media (e.g. the internet); increased importance of using social media to promote sport/sports performers.

■ Increased opportunities to experience sport via the media (e.g. 24-hour access via subscription channels) and availability of pay per view.

■ Increased media scrutiny of sports performers (they need to act appropriately).

■ Wider range of sports covered via the media (e.g. minority sports; Paralympics).

■ Increased promotion of sports performers in the media — the creation of 'sports stars'.

■ Increased media control over sport (e.g. timings of events); sports coverage is very important to the media and TV stations often market themselves based on their 'sports offer'.

The changing status of amateur and professional performers

Characteristics of 'modern-day amateurs' include the following:

■ They tend to be of lower status (professionals are now higher status).

■ Some high-level performers are still not professional (e.g. gymnasts).

■ There has been a blurring of amateur/professional distinctions, with less likelihood of exclusions as society has become more **egalitarian**. Performance at the top level in most sports is now open to all.

■ Some amateurs receive funding to pay for such costs as training expenses (e.g. via the National Lottery). It could be argued that this enables them to train as full-time athletes in modern-day sport, but that they do not gain financially from Lottery funding. Does this mean they are still amateurs?

> **Egalitarian** refers to a belief in the principle that all people are equal and deserve equal rights and opportunities.

Many factors are responsible for the growth of professional sport/increased status of professional performers through to the modern day:

■ All classes can compete; social class is no longer a barrier to success.

■ People are now respected for their talents/efforts in reaching the top.

■ There are high rewards for professionals through media and sponsorship (e.g. footballers).

■ Professionals have more time to train (i.e. many are full-time professionals), leading to higher standards of performance than amateurs in the same sport.

■ Celebrity status, more media coverage and investment in sport have led to vast increases in the financial rewards available for sportsmen/women and many sports have become able to support more professional performers (e.g. tennis and football). Many professionals are very wealthy and able to afford big houses, expensive cars etc. Such materialism is highly valued in modern-day society.

■ Positive role models act as motivators for others to achieve in professional sport.

■ Money invested in sports enables events and the sports themselves to operate and survive commercially.

Factors affecting the emergence of elite female performers and officials in football

A number of sociocultural factors have led to an increase in opportunities for women to participate and progress through to elite level in football in modern-day society:

- **Equal opportunities** — more sports are generally available to women, and socially acceptable, including football. Legally, the Sex Discrimination Act 1975 has led to less discrimination in sport on the basis of gender.
- **Increased media coverage of women's football** — BT Sport provides live coverage of the Women's Super League (WSL).
- **More female roles models in football** — as performers, coaches and officials.
- **More provision via school PE programmes** — in National Curriculum PE lessons/via extracurricular opportunities.
- **Increased approval/encouragement and resource investment via the FA** — for example, the women's national teams at various levels are fully supported by the FA.
- **More clubs being formed** — at local as well as 'professional' levels (e.g. WSL 1+2).
- **Increased participation via more funding into the game** — at grassroots level as well as elite level.
- **More free time** — as the traditional domestic responsibility role has decreased for women.

While relatively small in number in relation to their male counterparts, female referees are now more common at different levels of the game, according to the FA. This leads to optimism, with elite role models in refereeing (e.g. Sian Massey-Ellis) for young girls to aspire to.

A number of possible reasons can be given to account for this increase in women refereeing football matches at an elite level:

- FA active involvement in women's football in a variety of roles, including officiating (e.g. via FA development and recruitment programmes that have targeted female referees and the creation of the 'Women's Referee Development Pathway').
- The FA National Referee Strategy (NRS) presented new frameworks and structures in 2016/17, which included separate classifications for men's and women's football, and a specific focus on referee recruitment and retention among female referees.
- Use of positive role models/mentors to encourage women to become football referees.
- FA Respect campaign, aiming to improve player conduct and behaviour towards all referees, including women.
- A general increase in equality in society and recognition of women's ability to officiate football matches at the highest levels of the game; legal support/legislation in place against sexism, for example the Sex Discrimination Act.

Factors affecting the emergence of elite female performers in tennis

The work of the Women's Tennis Association (WTA) — a global leader in women's professional sport — illustrates how tennis can be viewed as one of a few sports in which female professional performers play a significant part. As part of the battle in fighting pay differentials in tennis tournaments such as Wimbledon, a number of women decided to create their own tour away from the men's. The WTA developed its own professional circuit in the late twentieth century, which provided ground-breaking opportunities for women to play at the top level, eventually earning millions of pounds through tournament earnings and sponsorship deals. Billie Jean King became the first female athlete to earn £100,000 in a single year.

In the early twenty-first century, worldwide media coverage of women's elite tennis tournaments leads to more potential role models for girls, as well as large sponsorship deals.

Factors affecting the emergence of elite female performers in athletics

The treatment of women in athletics remained 'indifferent' at best through to the late twentieth century. Even at this relatively late stage in the century, women were still excluded from a number of events in the Olympics — for example, the marathon was not open to women until the Los Angeles Olympics in 1984. The triple jump and hammer were only introduced for women in Atlanta in 1996 and Sydney in 2000 respectively. Fortunately, the negative myths and stereotypes about the capabilities of elite-level female athletes continue to be challenged, while competitions such as the Diamond League enable female as well as male athletes to earn millions as a result of their talents.

Summary

After studying this topic you should be able to:
- understand how the 'golden triangle' influences the development of modern-day sport
- understand the changing status of amateur and professional sport performers
- understand the factors affecting the emergence of elite female performers and officials

The impact of sport on society and of society on sport
Sociological theory applied to equal opportunities

This section of the specification introduces you to a number of key sociological terms, as well as considering the benefits of physical activity to the individual and wider society.

Sociological terms defined

Society

A human society is a group of people involved in frequent interpersonal relationships. This often involves a large social grouping sharing the same geographical territory.

Socialisation

Socialisation is a lifelong process in which members of a society learn its norms, values and beliefs in order to take their place in that society.

Primary socialisation

This occurs during the early years of childhood and takes place mainly within the immediate family (e.g. mother, father, siblings).

For many families, exercise provides a time when they come together, whether it be a shared involvement in an activity such as cycling or a family commitment to a member of the family who has devoted themselves to regular involvement in sporting competition.

Secondary socialisation

This occurs during the later years (e.g. as teenagers/adults), when the family is less involved and other 'agencies' are deliberately set up for the socialisation process and begin to exert more and more influence (e.g. peer groups, friends, schools).

Within this, gender socialisation involves the learning of behaviour and attitudes historically considered appropriate for a given sex. Participation in sport/physical activity can help create a 'social identity'. For example, participation can socialise boys/girls into 'traditional gender roles' of masculinity and femininity, which can influence the activities they participate in.

Social processes

This refers to forms of social interaction taking place between individuals and groups, which occur again and again.

Social control

This refers to the way in which people's thoughts, feelings, appearance and behaviour are regulated in social systems.

Social change

Social change is an alteration in the social order of society, i.e. significant changes in social behaviours and/or cultural values over time, leading to long-term effects. Sporting activities can be used (e.g. via specialist programmes) to try to bring about social change in a positive way. For example, 'This Girl Can' is a scheme trying to bring about social change in the way women's participation in physical activity is viewed.

Social issues

These are problems/conflicts that affect considerable numbers in society, for example disability/drug abuse/poor health linked to limited activity.

Inequality

This refers to the unfair situation in which resources/opportunities are distributed unequally within a society.

Social stratification

Social stratification is a form of social inequality in which society is divided into different levels/strata based on social class and/or wealth:

- Disposable income status can impact on participation in a positive/negative way.
- High-income earners can afford a wider variety of sports (e.g. expensive ones such as equestrianism), in contrast to low-income earners who have more restricted opportunities.
- High-income earners are able to afford a healthy diet, which helps health/fitness levels as part of an overall healthy lifestyle. Low-income earners tend to purchase cheaper, less healthy options.
- Social stratification can affect which sports are traditionally participated in, for example the middle class are associated with hockey and tennis, and the working class with boxing and rugby league.

Social action theory

This is way of viewing socialisation, emphasising the active roles people have in shaping society/social life, i.e. based on social actions such as our interactions and

Knowledge check 40

Using examples, explain what is meant by:

(a) primary socialisation

(b) secondary socialisation

negotiations with each other. Social action theory/the interactionist approach views sport and physical activity as a very important part of a society's make-up. Sport can impact on the social/cultural fabric of society and society can impact on sport. There are a number of ways in which sport can impact on society, including the following:

- By highlighting inequalities that exist between different social class groups (e.g. via the types of sports participated in linked to wealth/upbringing).
- By impacting on our beliefs concerning masculinity/femininity.
- By impacting on our ideas/beliefs about race/ethnicity (e.g. negatively through racist chanting targeted at footballers).
- By impacting on our ideas about ability and disability (e.g. positively through the achievements of Paralympians such as Jonnie Peacock).

Terms relating to the study of equality in sport are defined in Table 16.

Table 16 Key terms for the study of equality in sport

Target group	A section of society specifically aimed at because of its relative lack of involvement in sport (e.g. women/disabled/ethnic minority groups).
Channelling	A process whereby individuals may be pushed away from/into certain sports, based on assumptions made about them.
Equal opportunities	A term used in our society to emphasise inclusiveness and the importance of treating all people fairly, unhampered by artificial barriers, discrimination or prejudices.
Discrimination	The unfair treatment of a person or minority group; to make a distinction and act on a stereotype/prejudice. For example, a disabled individual may be denied access to a sports club because they are a wheelchair user, leading to less confidence/reduced sporting involvement.
Stereotyping	A standardised image/belief shared by society that makes simple generalisations about all members of a group, and which allows others to categorise and treat them accordingly. For example, some people may believe that women should not play certain sports, or sport at all. This can lead women to be channelled into certain sports and away from others (e.g. boxing).
Prejudice	An unfavourable opinion of an individual, often based on inadequate facts, for example lack of tolerance of or dislike of people from a specific race, religion or culture, which can negatively affect the treatment of a performer from an ethnic minority group by a coach.

Knowledge check 41

Consider the impact social stratification can have on sporting participation.

Knowledge check 42

Which of the following statements best defines the term 'discrimination'?

A Forming an unfavourable opinion of someone.

B Forming a standardised image of someone.

C The unfair situation where resources and opportunities are unevenly distributed within a society.

D The unfair treatment of a person or a minority group.

Exam tip

Avoid repeating terms already used in a question. For example, if a question asks for a definition of 'equal opportunities', avoid the word equal in your answer and use 'the same' instead.

The barriers to participation for under-represented groups in sport and physical activity

Barriers and solutions to sport/physical activity participation by the disabled, ethnic minority groups and women are outlined in Tables 17, 18 and 19 respectively.

Exam tip

For this section of the specification, it is important to develop your ability to understand and correctly interpret data/graphs relating to participation in sport and relate them to barriers/solutions/evaluation of solutions as appropriate.

Table 17 Common barriers and solutions to disability sport participation

Barriers	Solutions
Feedback — lack of specialist coaches to meet specific needs of disabled athletes	Increased training of specialist coaching (note there is still a lack of specialist coaches for disabled athletes)
Facilities — lack of access into and around some sports facilities, for example doorways are too narrow; some locations are difficult to travel to	Providing improved access into/around facilities; adaptive transport to facilities, for example taxis with ramps
Funding — relatively low income levels; costs of participation, for example membership fees and transport/specialist equipment; lack of sponsorship opportunities	Increased investment in disabled sport — subsidise it and make it more affordable, for example via local authority funding at all levels of disability sport (note the negative impact of local council spending cuts)
Feelings — negative self-image; low self-esteem; few role models/lack of media exposure	Providing more opportunities for success; helping talented athletes reach the highest levels possible and promoting them via increased media coverage; positive role models, for example Team GB Paralympic athletes (note there has been some improvement in the media profile of disability sport, but there is still a long way to go)
Factual awareness — lack of organised programmes/competitive sporting opportunities; lack of awareness of opportunities where they exist	Increase the amount/variety of competitive sporting opportunities, for example via local authority provision/Sport Development Officers/County Sport Partnerships; provide information via inclusive communications to access as many disabled individuals as possible using different formats, including social media
False viewpoints — negative myths/stereotypes about the capabilities of people with a disability; lower societal expectations; safety concerns — disability participation has traditionally been considered dangerous; negative stereotypes in disability sport may lead to discrimination, for example overt discrimination (e.g. verbal abuse)	Educating people on the myths/stereotypes about the capabilities of disabled athletes and challenging inappropriate attitudes; being more positive about the capabilities of disabled individuals in sport, for example via the work of specialist organisations (e.g. Activity Alliance)

Table 18 Common barriers and solutions to sport participation by ethnic minority groups

Barriers	Solutions
Racial stereotypes — fear of racist abuse, discrimination in society against black/Asian people; channelling into certain sports/away from others due to racial stereotypes	Organising campaigns against racism/discrimination in sport, for example, Kick it Out — football's equality and inclusion organisation — is working through the football, educational and community sectors to challenge discrimination and campaign for change
Culture — conflict with religious customs/cultural observances, for example dress (a particular concern with Muslim women)	Training more ethnic minority coaches, teachers and sports leaders, and educating them on the effects of racial stereotyping; ensuring there is single-sex provision, for example for Muslim women to overcome any cultural barriers to participation
Family — non-supportive family/parents; certain ethnic minority groups place a higher value on education as opposed to sporting participation	Educate ethnic minority/Asian parents on the value of sport in aiding personal/academic development of their children
Role models — fewer role models to aspire to, particularly in coaching/managerial positions	Promote positive ethnic minority role models where they exist, for example Nicola Adams (boxing); positive discrimination, for example the Football League and introduction of the **Rooney Rule** in the 2017/18 season to help recruit more ethnic minority coaches/managers into professional football
Low self-esteem — fear of rejection	Develop confidence via success/involvement at a local/community level, for example Street Games
Cost — low socioeconomic status of some ethnic minority groups may impact on participation patterns	Subsidise costs, for example via local authority schemes/Sport England initiatives (e.g. Sportivate)

The **Rooney Rule** is a national Football League policy that requires league teams to interview ethnic minority candidates for head coaching/senior football operation jobs.

Table 19 Common barriers and solutions to female sport participation

Barriers	Solutions
Stereotypes — negative myths are still evident in society, for example the belief that women lack aggression (e.g. for rugby)	Providing education/information about the capabilities of women to refute the stereotypical myths
Media — there is still far less media coverage of women's sport compared with men's; there are fewer attainable role models in sport for other women to aspire to, for example as coaches, officials or in positions of power (e.g. making decisions on national governing bodies)	Increased media coverage of women's sport; promote/provide more positive/attainable role models to aspire to
Funding — fewer opportunities for sponsorship or to become full-time sports performers; unequal pay	Increased sponsorship attracted to women's sport; provision of NGB central contracts to provide initial funding of full-time professional contracts, for example football (FA) and cricket (ECB)
PE — negative impact of school PE programmes, for example a lack of appealing activities to choose from	Improved PE provision, for example via a more varied choice of activity
Self-confidence — lack of fitness and body image issues lower self-confidence	Use social networking to connect women playing sport in order to create friendships with like-minded individuals and hopefully increase confidence/motivation to continue with it; provision of women-only sessions/beginners classes to help develop confidence
Opportunity — lack of income; continued stereotypes of traditional childcare role and/or domestic responsibilities	Encourage greater social acceptance of women having careers with more disposable income, giving them increased financial independence; encourage shared domestic/childcare responsibilities, creating more leisure time for women to participate
Channelling — women are encouraged into certain 'female-appropriate' activities (e.g. Zumba and badminton) and away from others (e.g. boxing and weightlifting); fewer clubs for women to join	Providing more opportunities for women to join sports clubs/participate in the activities they enjoy; increased acceptance via NGBs and their inclusivity/equal opportunities policies
Discrimination — this affects women in society, including sport, for example exclusion from membership of some clubs (e.g. golf)	Challenge discrimination, for example via laws — the Sex Discrimination Act 1975 makes sex discrimination unlawful

Benefits of increasing participation

Health and fitness benefits

- Regular weight-bearing exercise increases bone density, lowering the risk of osteoporosis in later life.
- Increased fitness/cardiovascular endurance through aerobic exercise. Reduced body weight decreases the risk of heart disease/stroke/type 2 diabetes.
- Increased joint flexibility as a result of regular stretching exercises reduces the risk of arthritis and maintains joint flexibility into later life.

Social benefits

- Doing physical activity/working with others improves communication/teamwork/cooperative skills/approachability; this increases opportunities to make friends with people with shared interests.
- As part of a weight loss plan for an overweight individual, sport and exercise can increase confidence to interact with others.

Exam tip

Make sure that you write answers linked to the specific benefits of the aspect of the specification contained in the question set — for example, health/fitness or social.

Knowledge check 43

Identify the social benefits to an individual of increasing their participation in physical activity.

Benefits to society of increased participation rates

- Increased health and fitness results in less strain on the NHS/decreased obesity.
- People participate together, leading to community integration/social cohesion.
- Keeping people out of trouble — those positively occupied in physical activity are less likely to commit crime.

Sport England partnerships aimed at increasing participation

Sport England has an overall mission reflected in its new strategy — 'Towards an Active Nation' (2016–21). It works with a range of partners locally and nationally to try to achieve its mission of increasing participation in sport/physical activity.

Local partners

One very important way in which Sport England achieves its mission is through working with local partners to meet local needs, for example **County Sports Partnerships (CSPs)**. The main aims of CSPs are to:

- increase adult participation in sport (e.g. via the 'Workplace Challenge')
- decrease the number of inactive adults
- get 1 million more young people active by 2020 (e.g. via School Games Festivals and local Sportivate projects)
- support and train more sports coaches (e.g. via local CSP databases/continuing professional development opportunities)

County Sports Partnerships (CSPs) are national networks of local agencies working together to increase numbers participating in sport and physical activity.

National partners

Sport England works directly with a number of nationally funded partners (Table 20).

Table 20 Sport England's national partners

National partners	Role in increasing participation in sport/physical activity
Child Protection in Sport Unit (CPSU)	Helps sports to safeguard children and young people in and through sport, for example by helping them to develop responses, structures and systems for safeguarding
Activity Alliance	Focuses on increasing activity in disabled people in sport and physical activity; its vision is to help ensure disabled people are active for life, for example via Get Out Get Active
Cricket Foundation	Delivers key programmes aimed at increasing opportunities for young people to play cricket, for example Chance to Shine/Street Chance; it allocates funding to grassroots/youth cricket
Football Foundation	A charity that directs £30 million into grassroots sport to deliver a programme of new and improved community sport facilities in towns and cities across England
Sporting Equals	Actively promoting greater involvement in sport/physical activity by all disengaged communities, such as the black and minority ethnic (BME) population; for example, the Making Equals project tries to engage diverse young people through sport, in order to break down barriers and empower them
Sports Aid	Works with NGBs to ensure that young, talented athletes are funded via cash awards during the critical early years of their careers, to ensure access to the best possible coaching and high-quality training facilities
Sports Coach UK	Support is given to help recruit, develop and retain the coaches needed to increase participation in sport, and help 'athletes' reach their performance goals
Sport and Recreation Alliance	Provides advice, support and guidance to its members, including those who represent NGBs and CSPs
Street Games	A national sports charity that brings sport to the doorsteps of young people in disadvantaged communities (e.g. Doorstep Sport)
Women in Sport	Helps sports bodies to engage more women and girls in sport; working with NGBs such as British Athletics, the national introduction of Parkrun has been highly successful in raising participation in women, as has been the development of a training online resource hub for CSPs

Summary

After studying this topic you should be able to:

- define key sociological issues in relation to your study of sport and explain their impact on equal opportunities in sport and society
- understand how social action theory relates to social issues in physical activity and sport
- understand the barriers to participation in sport and physical activity and the possible solutions to overcome such constraints for under-represented groups
- explain the health, fitness and social benefits of raising participation in sport and physical activity
- understand the cooperation between Sport England and its local and national partners in aiming to increase participation at grassroots level among under-represented groups in sport

Questions & Answers

This section explains the structure of AQA A-level Physical Education Paper 1 (7582) and discusses strategies for approaching the different types of questions you will encounter. This is followed by a series of sample questions covering all the question types — multiple choice, short answer and extended writing. Each question is followed by a sample student answer, with accompanying comments. You should practise all of these questions yourself and compare your answers with these, while reading the comments on the answers to improve your understanding of what is required to achieve full marks.

Exam format

Paper 1 of your PE A-level is divided into three sections to match the specification. In the exam each section is worth 35 marks and starts with a multiple-choice question. There are 12 marks available for short-answer questions (including multiple choice), and then there are two extended questions worth 8 marks and 15 marks. You have 2 hours to try to earn the 105 marks available. This paper counts for 35% of your A-level.

The extended-answer questions are marked using a levels-based scheme; some short-answer questions worth 6 marks can also be marked in this way. Your examiner will not just count up the number of AO1 marks (knowledge), AO2 marks (application/examples) and AO3 marks (analysis/evaluation). They will use a grid and highlight your answers using the following categories to come to an overall judgement:

- AO1 — knowledge
- AO2 — application
- AO3 — analysis/evaluation
- relevant terminology
- reasoning, clarity, structure and focus

(In the sample answers in this section, each assessment objective has been labelled **AO1**, **AO2** and **AO3**, so it is easier for you to see where the answer demonstrates knowledge, application and analysis/evaluation.)

For the 8-mark questions there are 2 marks available for AO1, 3 marks for AO2 and 3 marks for AO3. If no AO3 is evident at all in your answer, then a maximum of 5 marks only can be awarded.

For the 15-mark questions there are 4 marks available for AO1, 5 marks for AO2 and 6 marks for AO3. If no AO3 is evident at all in your answer, then a maximum of 9 marks only can be awarded.

Across Paper 1 and Paper 2 there will be two 15-mark questions and one 8-mark question that will be 'synoptic'. This means that the question could ask for any of the following:

- Knowledge, application and analysis/evaluation of two topics from the same section, for example:
  - Applied anatomy and physiology — the vascular system and the respiratory system
  - Skill acquisition — types of practice and operant conditioning
  - Sport and society — sports legislation and strategies to control crowd violence
- Knowledge, application and analysis/evaluation of two topics from different sections, for example:
  - Applied anatomy and physiology/Skill acquisition
  - Applied anatomy and physiology/Sport and society
  - Skill acquisition/Sport and society
- Knowledge, application and analysis/evaluation of one topic from any section in Paper 1 with another topic from any section in Paper 2.

If there is more than one topic in the question, try to link the topics where possible. If you do not do this, you will not be able to access the top level.

Finally, in the exam it is important that you write clearly in the spaces provided in the answer booklet. Avoid writing anything that you want to be marked in the margins and always indicate if you run out of space that your answer continues on additional paper.

Exam comments

Each question is followed by a brief analysis of what to watch out for when answering the question. All student responses are then annotated by examiner's comments, which indicate where credit is due. In the weaker answers, they also point out areas for improvement, specific problems and common errors, such as lack of clarity, weak or non-existent development, irrelevance, misinterpretation of the question and mistaken meanings of terms.

Applied anatomy and physiology

Cardiovascular system

Question 1

During a game of football, a defender will work at various intensities. Describe how cardiac output increases when a defender is working at high intensity in the match.   [4 marks]

For this question, remember the equation:

cardiac output = heart rate × stroke volume

Student A answer

In the match the player's cardiac output increases when it is high intensity due to the increase in impulses from the sympathetic nervous system ✓. This will send impulses to the SAN to increase its rate of firing ✓ so heart rate increases ✓. The heart will also have a stronger contraction ✓ and this will result in an increase in stroke volume ✓.

4/4 marks awarded This answer scores more than the maximum 4 marks. Student A has correctly identified how cardiac output increases. Alternative answers could have included increased levels of carbon dioxide, the release of adrenalin and an increased diastolic filling of the ventricles.

Student B answer

Cardiac output increases because the football defender needs more blood to go to their muscles, so they receive more oxygen. This will mean that the defender can work at higher intensities throughout the whole game.

0/4 marks awarded Student B has made a common error by not reading the question carefully and instead explains *why* cardiac output increases, not *how*. Always highlight the command term, so that you understand the requirements of the question.

Question 2

Explain the causes of the Bohr shift and identify the effect that this change has on oxygen delivery to the muscles.   [4 marks]

There are two parts to address — what causes the Bohr shift and how it affects oxygen delivery.

Student A answer

An increase in blood temperature ✓, an increase in the partial pressure of blood carbon dioxide ✓ and a low blood pH ✓ cause the Bohr shift. These all result in oxygen dissociating quickly and more readily from haemoglobin ✓.

4/4 marks awarded Student A has addressed both parts of the question, correctly identifying the causes of the Bohr shift and that it causes the dissociation of oxygen from haemoglobin to occur more readily and thus increases oxygen uptake.

Student B answer

There are three factors that cause the Bohr shift. These are an increase in blood carbon dioxide ✓, an increase in blood temperature ✓ and a low blood pH caused by more carbon dioxide ✓.

3/4 marks awarded Student B has only addressed one part of the question. This is a common mistake in exams. If there is more than one part to a question highlight them, because often when answering the first part students forget about the second or even third part and then move on to the next question.

Question 3

Define the arterio-venous oxygen difference (A-VO₂ diff) and explain what happens to this difference following the onset of exercise.

[2 marks]

You need to do two things: define the term and explain what happens during exercise.

Student A answer

The arterio-venous oxygen difference is the difference in oxygen content between the arterial blood arriving at the muscles and the venous blood leaving the muscles ✓. During exercise this difference increases because there is a greater uptake of oxygen by the muscles ✓.

2/2 marks awarded Student A has addressed both parts of the question, correctly defining the arterio-venous oxygen difference and then explaining that it increases and why this occurs.

Student B answer

The arterio-venous difference is the difference in oxygen content between the atria and the ventricles.

0/2 marks awarded Student B has made the common mistake of thinking that the arterio-venous oxygen difference refers to the chambers of the heart rather than the blood vessels. He has also forgotten to answer the second half of the question. Always read questions carefully and check that you have an answer to each part.

Respiratory system

Question 4

In order to make use of their stamina, footballers need to take in oxygen. The diagram below shows values for the partial pressure of oxygen and carbon dioxide at two different locations in one gas exchange system.

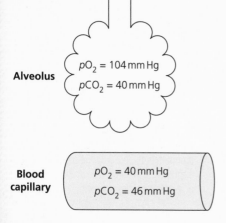

Alveolus
$pO_2 = 104\,\text{mm Hg}$
$pCO_2 = 40\,\text{mm Hg}$

Blood capillary
$pO_2 = 40\,\text{mm Hg}$
$pCO_2 = 46\,\text{mm Hg}$

Use the information from the diagram to explain how oxygen and carbon dioxide move between the two locations. [4 marks]

> You need to make sure that diffusion is defined and the movement of both gases is mentioned using the values from the diagram. A typical mistake in gaseous exchange questions is to just include oxygen in your answer and omit carbon dioxide.

Student A answer

Both oxygen and carbon dioxide move between the alveoli and blood capillaries through diffusion, which is where a gas moves from an area of high concentration to an area of low concentration ✓. Oxygen moves from the alveolus, where it is at a high concentration (104 mmHg) to the blood capillary ✓, where it is at a low concentration (40 mmHg) ✓. Carbon dioxide on the other hand moves in the opposite direction from the blood capillary ✓, where it is at a high concentration (46 mmHg) to the alveolus, where it is at a low concentration (40 mmHg) ✓.

4/4 marks awarded Student A has made more than enough marking points, and correctly identified diffusion and defined it. The values in the diagram are then used to explain how both oxygen and carbon dioxide move between the two locations.

Student B answer

Diffusion takes place. Oxygen moves from the alveolus to the blood capillary and carbon dioxide from the blood capillary to the alveolus ✓.

1/4 marks awarded Student B has not defined diffusion and has not used the values from the diagram to explain that both oxygen and carbon dioxide move from an area of high concentration to an area of low concentration.

Question 5

Identify which **one** of the following statements is correct. [1 mark]

A Tidal volume is the amount of air breathed in after a normal breath

B Expiratory reserve volume is the amount of air that can be breathed out

C Minute ventilation is inspiratory reserve volume + expiratory reserve volume

D Inspiratory reserve volume is the amount of air that can be forcibly inspired after a normal breath

> There will be multiple-choice questions in your exam. Follow the instructions on how to answer these very carefully.

Student A answer

D Inspiratory reserve volume is the amount of air that can be forcibly inspired after a normal breath

1/1 mark awarded For multiple-choice questions, make sure to completely fill in the circle alongside the appropriate answer. Check that all parts of a definition are present.

Student B answer

D Inspiratory reserve volume is the amount of air that can be forcibly inspired after a normal breath

0/1 mark awarded Although Student B has identified the correct answer, she has not followed the instructions. On your exam paper you have to fill in the circle because the question is scanned and not marked by examiners.

Neuromuscular system

Question 6

Proprioceptive neuromuscular facilitation (PNF) will be part of a training programme for an elite gymnast. Explain the role of the muscle spindles and Golgi tendon organs in PNF stretching, and justify why a gymnast might choose to do PNF as part of their training programme.

[8 marks]

This is an extended-response question, so will be marked using the levels-based scheme. You need to make sure that you demonstrate your knowledge of PNF, apply it to muscle spindles and Golgi tendon organs, and analyse why it is relevant for a gymnast.

Student A answer

Using the CRAC technique A01, PNF stretching involves passively stretching the muscle first A01. The stretch is detected by muscle spindles A02 and impulses are sent through the CNS to cause the stretch reflex A02. This occurs to prevent over stretching A02. The aim of PNF is to override the stretch reflex A01.

Golgi tendon organs are activated when there is tension in a muscle. A02 This occurs when the muscle is then contracted isometrically in PNF A01 and the Golgi tendon organs sense the increase in muscle tension and send inhibitory signals to the brain A02. This causes the antagonist muscles to relax, so autogenic inhibition occurs A02 and allows greater range of movement A02.

Flexibility is really important for a gymnast. PNF is considered one of the most effective methods for increasing the range of motion around a joint A03 and it can also strengthen the joint A03. Regular training using PNF will increase the aesthetic quality of the gymnast's performance A03.

7/8 marks awarded Student A addresses all A01, A02 and A03 areas. The answer has the required breadth and depth, with relevant terminology throughout, and is written clearly with relevant focus, so will be awarded a mark from level 4.

Student B answer

PNF improves flexibility A01. A stretch is detected by the muscle spindles and this can cause the stretch reflex A02. Next, the performer does an isometric contraction A01 so that Golgi tendon organs are activated; these inhibit the stretch reflex, which means the gymnast can stretch further A02.

3/8 marks awarded This answer is too vague and does not have enough depth, for example Student B writes that a stretch is performed, but does not identify the type of stretch as passive. There is not enough justification evident as to why a gymnast might use PNF, so there are no A03 marks awarded.

Movement analysis

Question 7

Evaluate the importance of a sagittal plane and transverse axis during a game for a rugby player.

[8 marks]

Make sure that you cover all three assessment objectives. First, show as much knowledge as you can about the sagittal plane and transverse axis (AO1), then apply it and give examples in a game of rugby when joint actions in this plane and axis are used (AO2). Finally, evaluate the use of the sagittal plane and transverse axis (AO3). Are these the only plane and axis used during the game?

Student A answer

The sagittal plane divides the body into right and left halves **AO1** and a transverse axis runs from side to side across the body **AO1**. Flexion, extension, hyperextension, plantar flexion and dorsi flexion are the joint actions that occur in a sagittal plane and transverse axis **AO1**. In a game of rugby, as the player runs with the ball, flexion and extension occur at the knee joint in both the drive and recovery leg **AO2**. In addition, as the rugby player pushes off the ground, they plantar flex their ankle joint **AO2**. They also use the sagittal plane and axis when they kick the ball **AO2**. As they prepare to kick, they hyperextend the hip and flex the knee **AO2**. As they perform the kick, they flex the hip, and if they kick on their laces, they plantar flex the ankle **AO2**.

Although the sagittal plane and transverse axis are important, they are not the only plane and axis that are used during a game of rugby **AO3**. When the player passes the ball, the shoulders abduct and adduct horizontally, and these joint actions occur in a transverse plane and longitudinal axis **AO3**. In addition, as a tackle is made, the player will abduct their shoulders as they reach around the player they are tackling **AO3**. Abduction occurs in a frontal plane and sagittal axis **AO3**.

8/8 marks awarded Student A has addressed all the assessment objectives, explaining the plane and axis and identifying the joint actions, applying them to relevant examples in a game of rugby. Evaluation of other planes and axes used in rugby means that AO3 marks can be awarded.

Student B answer

Flexion, extension, hyperextension, plantar flexion and dorsi flexion occur in a sagittal plane and transverse axis **AO1**. The sagittal plane divides the body into right and left halves **AO1** and a transverse axis runs from side to side across the body **AO1**. When running with the ball, flexion and extension occur in the hips and the knees, with plantar flexion and dorsi flexion in the ankle **AO2**. As a kick is executed the hip flexes, the knee extends and the ankle plantar flexes **AO2**. Also, when the player passes the ball, the elbows extend **AO2**. All these joint actions during the game take place in a sagittal plane and transverse axis.

5/8 marks awarded Student B cannot access a mark higher than 5 because she has not addressed AO3. When answering an extended question, it is worth annotating your answer with AO1, AO2 and AO3 in the margin, so that you can check that you have addressed all the assessment objectives.

Question 8

Identify which **one** of the following statements is incorrect. [1 mark]

A The articulating bones of the shoulder are the scapula and humerus

B The articulating bones of the ankle are the tibia, fibula and talus

C The articulating bones of the elbow are the humerus, radius and ulna

D The articulating bones of the knee are the femur, tibia and fibula

> With all multiple-choice questions, look at the choices carefully and take your time. Do not rush into a decision.

Student A answer

D The articulating bones of the knee are the femur, tibia and fibula

> **1/1 mark awarded** Student A correctly identifies that D is the incorrect answer because the fibula is not an articulating bone in the knee.

Student B answer

B The articulating bones of the ankle are the tibia, fibula and talus

> **0/1 mark awarded** In the ankle all of these bones are correct. Questions that are simple recall of knowledge should be easy to answer with thorough revision.

Energy systems

Question 9

An endurance performer needs to have a good VO_2 max in order to be successful. Explain the factors that contribute to a good VO_2 max, and evaluate whether altitude training is an appropriate method for improving an endurance performer's VO_2 max. [15 marks]

> This is a 15-mark extended question, so you need to make as many AO1, AO2 and AO3 comments as you can. Show your understanding of VO_2 max and altitude training first, then apply them with examples related to endurance running, and finally evaluate or justify.

Student A answer

Altitude training occurs at over 1500 m above sea level **A01** — performers need to remain at altitude for a decent period of time, such as a month, so they can acclimatise **A01**. At altitude the partial pressure of oxygen is lower, so there is less oxygen available **A01**. VO_2 max is the maximum volume of oxygen that can be taken up and used by the muscles per minute **A01**.

An endurance runner needs a good VO_2 max and altitude training can help this happen. By training at altitude, an endurance performer will increase their number of red blood cells A02. This increases the oxygen carrying capacity of the blood A02 so their muscles receive more oxygen and, consequently, it increases their VO_2 max A02. Also, altitude training increases the amount of myoglobin the endurance runner will have, so more oxygen can be stored during their performance A02 and they will have more mitochondria, so more aerobic respiration can take place, which is needed for their event A02. An endurance runner with a good VO_2 max will need an increase in myoglobin and mitochondria so that more oxygen can be taken up and used at the muscle site A03. A good VO_2 max is also genetically based, i.e. it can be inherited A01, and a male endurance runner may have a higher VO_2 max than a female endurance runner A02.

Although altitude training is a suitable training method for improving VO_2 max, it is not accessible to everyone A03 because it is very expensive A03 and an individual has to spend a considerable time at altitude, so this could lead to being homesick A01. Also, altitude training will not improve VO_2 max straight away, and an endurance performer could experience altitude sickness and this could prevent them from training at the same level of intensity for the first week or so A03. It is possible for an endurance performer to use an alternative method that has the same effects and is more accessible and cheaper, such as an altitude tent A03.

13/15 marks awarded This answer covers all assessment objectives and would score in the top band. Student A has made good links between altitude training and VO_2 max. He has also explained how altitude training can help improve VO_2 max due to the adaptations that take place and how these improve performance.

Student B answer

VO_2 max is the maximum volume of oxygen that can be taken in per minute. Altitude training occurs over high ground where the air is thinner, so there is less oxygen available for the working muscles A01. This means that anyone training at altitude has to work harder at first and then they will gain benefits such as more mitochondria and more myoglobin A01. It also increases the number of red blood cells A01 and the amount of EPO A01.

However, altitude training can cause altitude sickness A01 and also when a performer first goes up to altitude that fact there is less oxygen means they cannot work as hard, so detraining takes place and therefore there could be a loss of fitness A01. Having to train at altitude could also result in being homesick because you are away from home in a strange place A01.

4/15 marks awarded Definitions have to be accurate, and the VO_2 max definition here was not accurate enough. In addition, there were no links made between altitude training and VO_2 max, and there was no application to an endurance performer. All the comments were knowledge based and therefore only A01 marks could be awarded.

Question 10

During the winter season, many athletes compete indoors. Sprinters compete over 60 metres. Explain how the majority of energy is produced during a 60-metre sprint.   [3 marks]

This question requires an explanation of one of the three energy systems. Use the intensity and duration of the 60 m sprint to decide which energy system it is.

Student A answer

The majority of energy is provided using the ATP-PC system ✓ because the 60 m sprint is a short-duration, high-intensity event. This system is anaerobic ✓, where the enzyme creatine kinase ✓ breaks down phosphocreatine into phosphate and creatine ✓. There is enough energy resynthesised to create 1 ATP ✓.

3/3 marks awarded This answer makes more than enough scoring points. Student A has correctly identified that energy is produced using the ATP-PC system and then explained the key points of this system. She could also have mentioned that aerobic energy is needed for recovery.

Student B answer

During the 60 m sprint, the athlete uses the anaerobic glycolytic system to produce energy. It is anaerobic and occurs in the sarcoplasm. PFK is the enzyme that is responsible for glycolysis, where glycogen is converted to glucose-6-phosphate and broken down to pyruvic acid.

Pyruvic acid is then converted to lactic acid and 2 ATP are produced.

0/3 marks awarded Student B has identified an incorrect energy system, so even though he has explained this system perfectly, no marks can be awarded. Always look at the intensity and duration of the sporting example, which will help you to decide which energy system is the predominant one for producing energy.

■ Skill acquisition

Skill, skill continua and transfer of skills

Question 1

Classify the skill of sending a pass in ice hockey on the following continua:

Open————————Closed

Discrete————————Serial————————Continuous

Simple————————Complex

Justify your answers. [3 marks]

> In order to access all 3 marks you must justify your answers. Each part of your answer must relate to an ice hockey pass.

Student A answer

The ice hockey pass can be classified as open, discrete and complex. It is an open skill because the environment around the player is constantly changing. Their team mates are continually moving around the ice ✓ in order to get into position to receive the pass, and the opposition is also moving in order to block/intercept. The player must adapt.

The pass is also discrete because it has a clear beginning when the stick is swung backwards preparing to hit the puck, and a clear ending when the player finishes the follow through with their stick ✓.

Finally, the pass is complex because the player has to make several decisions in order to complete the pass, including who to pass to ✓, where defenders are, and the direction, speed and power of the pass.

3/3 marks awarded Student A has correctly identified the classification of the skill, and has clearly justified their answer with practical application back to the ice hockey pass. It is a well-structured answer with three short paragraphs.

Student B answer

The pass is open, complex and discrete.

0/3 marks awarded Student B has correctly identified the skill on all three continua. However, she has not justified her answer and as a result fails to score any marks.

Question 2

Identify which **one** of the following statements describes negative transfer. [1 mark]

A Negative transfer is when one skill aids the learning and performance of another skill

B Negative transfer is when you learn to perform a skill on the left side of the body and then do the same on the right side of the body

C   Negative transfer is when there are no transferrable elements between two skills

D   Negative transfer is when one skill hinders the learning and performance of another skill

> There will be multiple-choice questions in your exam. Ensure that you follow the instructions on how to answer this type of question very carefully.

Student A answer

D   Negative transfer is when one skill hinders the learning and performance of another skill.

1/1 mark awarded This answer is correct. Make sure you learn the definitions of the four types of transfer carefully.

Student B answer

D   Negative transfer is when one skill hinders the learning and performance of another skill

0/1 mark awarded Although the student has identified the correct answer, he has not followed the instructions. On your exam paper you cannot cross or tick the answer — you have to completely fill in the circle because the question is scanned and not marked by examiners.

Impact of skill classification on structure of practice for learning

Question 3

Using examples from invasion games, describe variable and mental practice.   [4 marks]

> This question requires you to describe both types of practice and give an example from an invasion game to illustrate each one.

Student A answer

Variable practice means that the player will practise a skill such as chest passing in basketball in a range of situations ✓ that become more and more competitive. This could be static chest passing with a partner, then chest passing while on the move, then passing with a passive defender and finally a 2 v 1 mini game ✓.

Mental practice means that the player will go through the movement patterns of the skill in their head, but they don't actually move ✓, although the signals are sent to the correct parts of the body that will produce the action. For example, just before a rugby player takes the conversion kick, they stand still and close their eyes. In their mind, they see themselves taking the kick and scoring the conversion ✓. Their brain will still send a signal to the quadriceps and gastrocnemius, but they don't contract.

4/4 marks awarded This is an excellent answer that clearly describes both types of practice and gives clear practical examples from basketball and rugby, which are both invasion games.

Variable practice is where the performer varies the skill they are practising. Mental practice is where the performer mentally practises the skill. For example, in badminton they would see themselves doing a powerful smash.

0/4 marks awarded Student B has attempted to address both types of practice but has not scored with their answer. 'Varies' is a repeat of the question term 'variable'. The answer needs to describe the method by using other words to suggest that the practice drills change. There has been no attempt at an example of variable practice. For mental practice, he has repeated the question term again. He has offered a sound example to support his answer. However, badminton is a net/wall game, not an invasion game, so the examiner is unable to give credit.

Principles and theories of learning and performance

Question 4

Bandura suggests that performers learn through observation. Describe how a performer would learn to dribble in hockey, with reference to the attention and motivation parts of his model.

[4 marks]

This question requires a deep understanding of Bandura's model. You need to apply your knowledge to get all the marks on offer. Show how the 'attention' and 'motivation' parts of the model would help a performer to learn to dribble.

Student A answer

Bandura states that the performer must pay attention and be motivated in order to learn to dribble. The hockey player should focus on the key aspects ✓ of the skill. The coach can highlight the main parts. For example, the coach will point out exactly where the player's hands should be ✓ as they grip the hockey stick. In addition, the player must be driven ✓ to learn how to dribble and have the desire to practise the skill of dribbling ✓.

4/4 marks awarded Both parts of the model have been correctly described and an example related to dribbling in hockey given to support each answer. It is clear that Student A understands Bandura's model.

Student B answer

Bandura says that the performer must pay attention to the stick and ball. This means they have to remember how the dribble is supposed to be done and have a clear mental image of the dribble. The performer must really want ✓ to do the skill too.

1/4 marks awarded This answer shows that Student B has some understanding of Bandura's model but does not appear to have revised enough. She has written about remembering/having a clear mental image of the skill, which relates to a different part of the model (retention). This is a common mistake. No mark can be offered for the example here. She scrapes 1 mark for describing motivation, but has not offered an example, so no further credit can be given.

Question 5

A hockey player has recently joined a team and has become increasingly more proficient in her skills. Using an example from hockey, describe the associative stage of learning.

[4 marks]

> This question requires a description of the associative stage only, and you must give an example from hockey to support your answer.

Student A answer

The hockey player has continually practised ✓ her dribbling ✓ skills in order to progress from the cognitive phase. Her dribbling is much smoother ✓ and she can start to look up a bit to the other players in her surrounding environment ✓ rather than just focusing on the ball. If she doesn't practise regularly, she might not progress on to the next stage, which would make her autonomous.

> **4/4 marks awarded** Student A has written an excellent answer. He has given more than three correct descriptive points of the associative stage, and used a simple but effective example from hockey, as requested.

Student B answer

She makes fewer mistakes when playing hockey. She starts to develop the kinaesthesis ✓ of the movements. She might not go any further.

> **1/4 marks awarded** Student B has made some attempt to answer the question and has scored 1 mark with a correct technical word. However, making fewer mistakes is referred to in the question ('more proficient'), and therefore cannot be credited. 'When playing hockey' is also too vague to gain the example point — the answer should refer to a named skill, for example passing or shooting, and link it to a description of the associative phase.

Use of guidance and feedback

Question 6

Identify which **one** of the following statements is an example of manual guidance.

[1 mark]

A   The performer watches a video of a footballer passing

B   The coach stands behind the golfer with his arms around him. He places his hands on top of the golfer's and supports his swing

C   A young boy uses stabilisers on his new bike

D   A tennis coach explains how to successfully perform the drop shot

> Multiple-choice questions may appear to be easy, but they can be tricky. Do not rush into answering — read the question several times before you shade in the circle.

Student A answer

B   The coach stands behind the golfer with his arms around him. He places his hands on top of the golfer's and supports his swing

1/1 mark awarded Student A has correctly identified the example of manual guidance. Make sure that you can describe all four types and give clear sporting examples of each.

Student B answer

C   A young boy uses stabilisers on his new bike

0/1 mark awarded Student B has answered incorrectly. He has made the common mistake of confusing manual guidance with mechanical guidance.

Memory models: general information processing model

Question 7

A gymnast performing on a beam has to use selective attention because her competitors are performing on other pieces of apparatus in the competition venue at the same time. With reference to gymnastics, describe what selective attention is and explain how it benefits the performer.

[4 marks]

There are several things to address in this question. You must describe selective attention and give an example that relates to gymnastics. To access all the marks, you must then explain the benefits of selective attention.

Student A answer

Selective attention acts as an information filter. The performer will focus on the relevant stimuli in the environment and disregard the irrelevant information ✓. The gymnast will only be focusing on landing her moves on the beam and will completely ignore the other performers on the floor/vault etc. and the shouts from the crowd ✓. This will benefit her because it will control her arousal/anxiety levels ✓ and stop her from becoming distracted ✓. She will be able to fully concentrate.

4/4 marks awarded Student A has clearly described selective attention and has given a clear example relating to gymnastics, as required by the question. Finally, she has explained a number of benefits and have therefore accessed all the available marks.

Student B answer

The gymnast will selectively attend so that she focuses on the beam and not on the gymnast next to her on the uneven bars ✓. This will benefit her because she will not experience information overload ✓.

2/4 marks awarded This answer scores half the available marks. Typically, this student has not addressed all parts of the question — he has not described selective attention. This is a common mistake in exams. Make sure you highlight the questions so that you address each part before moving on. Student B has given a good example and one benefit. To access all the marks, more benefits of selective attention should have been given.

Memory models: efficiency of information processing

Question 8

Using practical examples, describe the functions of the perceptual and effector mechanisms in Whiting's model.

[2 marks]

> This question requires you to have knowledge and understanding of Whiting's model and also to be able to apply your knowledge to practical examples. The terminology often scares students, so revise all aspects of her model thoroughly — it is often easier than it first appears.

Student A answer

The perceptual mechanism is where the DCR process (detection, comparison, recognition) and selective attention happens. All the relevant information is separated from the irrelevant information. For example, during a tennis serve the player should focus on the ball and ignore the crowd ✓.

The effector mechanism sends impulses to the muscles needed to produce the movement. In the tennis serve, impulses will be sent from the brain to the muscles of the arms and shoulders, for example the biceps and deltoids, so that the racquet can be swung to serve ✓.

2/2 marks awarded This answer easily scores both marks because the functions of the perceptual and effector mechanisms have been clearly described and examples for each given to support the answer. Student A chose to give examples from tennis, but since the question does not specify a sport he could have chosen any. It is always best to relate examples to skills you know best — think about you and your own performance.

Student B answer

The perceptual mechanism interprets the information through the DCR process and then filters the relevant information from the irrelevant information, for example when a footballer takes a penalty he is able to focus on the ball and the goal and completely disregard the crowd behind the goal who are trying to distract him ✓.

The effector mechanism sends electrical impulses from the brain to the working muscles via the nervous system.

1/2 marks awarded Student B shows a good understanding of Whiting's model. The description of the perceptual mechanism is accurate and the example of what the performer will focus on is clear. Technical terminology is also used. The effector mechanism is also accurately described. However, there is no example of this and therefore no second mark.

Question 9

Define simple and choice reaction time.

[2 marks]

> This is a very straightforward definition question. Ensure that you can clearly distinguish between simple and choice reaction time.

Student A answer

Simple reaction time is where the performer is presented with one stimulus and there is only one possible response ✓, for example in the 100 m sprint the sound of the gun is the stimulus and the response is to run.

Choice reaction time is where there are multiple stimuli and also multiple possible responses ✓, for example in hockey several of your team mates are shouting for you to pass them the ball and you have to choose who to pass to.

2/2 marks awarded Student A has given clear definitions of both simple and choice reaction times. She has also supported their definitions with accurate sporting examples, even though she is not required to do so. This is good practice.

Student B answer

Simple reaction time is when the performer has few decisions to make. Choice reaction time is slower because the performer has lots of decisions to make.

0/2 marks awarded Student B has misinterpreted the question. He appears to have given the definitions of simple and complex skills. Read the question carefully.

Question 10

Describe the whole method of presentation. With reference to performers' experience and skill classification, evaluate its effectiveness when developing skills.

[15 marks]

> For this 15-mark extended question you need to access as many A01, A02 and A03 marks as you can. Remember that this is a banded-mark question, so your answer is considered holistically. Show your knowledge of the whole method of presentation. Identify, classify and justify sporting skills and evaluate how effective the whole method would be in developing them.

Student A answer

The whole method of presentation means that the skill is not broken down into its subroutines **A01**. It is presented in its entirety **A01**. The whole method could be used with highly organised skills that are difficult to break down into subroutines **A01**, such as the golf swing **A02**. It can also be used with continuous skills, which do not have a clear beginning and ending **A01**, such as cycling **A02**. Simple skills such as the forward roll **A02** can be presented in their entirety because there are few decisions to make **A01** when performing.

It is advantageous to use the whole method with highly organised skills because it maintains fluency A03 between the subroutines of the skill, for example the full tennis serve rather than parts such as the ball toss A02, which ensures that kinaesthesis A03 is developed. It is not time consuming A03, so a full tennis serve can be produced in a small amount of time, and it enables the performer to develop a clear mental image A03 of what the tennis serve should look like.

However, it is difficult to use with cognitive performers A03, so other methods should be utilised. It can be used effectively with autonomous performers because they have a good understanding of the skill as a whole, for example an autonomous sprinter knows what to do in the sprint start A02 and can produce it fully each time. It is also quite fatiguing A03 to repeatedly produce the full skill — for example, you would be extremely tired having to do a full somersault A02 over and over; therefore the performer must be physically capable of producing the full skill A03.

15/15 marks awarded This answer covers all the assessment objectives and would score in the top band. Student A has accurately described the whole method of presentation. He has classified and justified several sporting skills that would be best presented using the whole method. He has evaluated the method, giving clear advantages and disadvantages that explain its effectiveness.

Student B answer

This means the skill is presented as one A01, for example showing a full cartwheel A02. A cartwheel is hard to break down into parts because it is highly organised A01. It is a quick to use A03.

The whole method should be used if the skill does not have a definite start and end A01 because it is cyclic, for example the badminton smash.

4/15 marks awarded This is a weak answer. Evidence of knowledge of the whole method is limited and there is very little application to sporting situations. A very basic analysis point is made; other than this there is no analysis/evaluation.

■ Sport and society

Characteristics of popular recreation in pre-industrial Britain (pre-1780)

Question 1

Which **one** of the following social classes participated in real tennis in pre-industrial Britain? [1 mark]

A   Middle class

B   Working class

C   Lower class

D   Upper class

> Do not confuse real tennis with lawn tennis, which developed in the post-industrial era.

Student A answer

D   Upper class

1/1 mark awarded The correct social class identified.

Student B answer

A   Middle class

0/1 mark awarded The middle class were associated with lawn tennis in the post-industrial era.

Question 2

Explain how social class influenced sporting recreation in pre-industrial Britain.   [4 marks]

> This question requires you to explain clearly how and why lower-class members of society participated in certain sports, and upper-class individuals took part in others of a totally different nature.

Student A answer

Social class strongly influenced participation in pre-industrial Britain, with lower-class people playing certain sports such as mob football very occasionally due to their very long working hours ✓. With very little development of transport or communications at this time, it meant the lower class could only play sport in the local areas they lived in ✓.

In contrast to this, the upper class were the leisured class, with lots of free time to play sports such as real tennis on a regular basis ✓. They also had the ability to travel, so could play real tennis against opponents in other parts of the country (i.e. it was non-local) ✓.

4/4 marks awarded This is a very well-balanced answer, which addresses both social class groups of the time and directly explains, in a number of different ways, how they impacted on sports participation in mob football and real tennis.

Student B answer

Class influenced sporting recreation in pre-industrial Britain because certain violent sports were played by the lower class, such as mob football, which reflected their cruel/harsh lifestyles ✓. It was also played in rural areas locally as the lower class lived in the countryside ✓.

2/4 marks awarded The answer focuses on one part of the question (i.e. the lower class) and does not address the influence of the upper class.

Industrial and post-industrial development of sport (1780–1900)

Question 3

Explain why national governing bodies of sport emerged in the second half of the nineteenth century.

[4 marks]

This question requires you to identify and explain a number of important developments within sport in nineteenth-century Britain, which led to NGBs emerging, such as the FA (1863).

Student A answer

There was a need for organisations to standardise rules for sports across the whole of the country, i.e. codification for the nation ✓. There was also a need for organisations to be set up that clubs could join, such as the FA for the large numbers of football clubs being formed ✓. With more clubs being formed and playing more regularly, an organisation was needed to organise competitions for them, such as the Football League ✓. Some sports (e.g. Rugby Union) required an organisation to be set up (e.g. the RFU) to control eligibility, i.e. who was allowed to play their sport ✓.

4/4 marks awarded This is a good clear answer, which correctly explains four reasons why NGBs emerged in the nineteenth century.

Student B answer

More clubs formed as sports like football became more popular and they needed an organisation to affiliate to ✓. There was also a need for an organisation to come up with a single set of rules for playing a sport, i.e. codification ✓. There was also a need to control the development of sports.

2/4 marks awarded This gives two good explanations of factors influencing the emergence of NGBs, but the final reason is simply stated and not explained.

Question 4

Discuss the impact of the Industrial Revolution on working-class sport during the industrial and post-industrial period (1780–1900).

[8 marks]

This requires you to identify and explain a number of ways in which industrialisation initially impacted negatively on sporting opportunities for the working class before describing how it eventually provided more opportunities for them to play and watch sport.

Student A answer

The Industrial Revolution had both a positive and a negative effect on the development of sport, as I will discuss below.

In relation to money and time, initially it was negative A01 because the working class worked very long hours for very low pay, meaning limited spare income, time and energy to play sport A02. However, as the nineteenth century progressed, various laws were passed reducing working hours and giving the workers more rights, including paid holidays and more free time to spend playing and watching sport A03. In the late eighteenth century, as the Industrial Revolution occurred, living and working conditions were very poor A01 with very poor health among the working class, meaning they had little desire/energy to play sport A02. However, as the nineteenth century progressed many kind middle-class factory owners improved working conditions and sometimes provided housing and sports facilities for their workers (e.g. Titus Salt in Saltaire) A03. This had a very positive impact on the development of sport as the working class became fitter and more willing to get involved in sport A03. Finally, you could argue that, without the Industrial Revolution, modern-day sports such as association football would not have emerged without the ability to manufacture sports equipment such as footballs, nets and goal posts A03.

7/8 marks awarded Information on a range of relevant points is consistently accurate, with analysis/ evaluation evident as each point is made. There is a clear structure/focus to the answer, which uses relevant terms throughout and addresses all three assessment objectives.

Student B answer

The Industrial Revolution was good for working-class sport. It meant that workers had more free time to play and watch sport `A01`. This was due to Factory Acts being passed as laws, one of which meant that workers were free on Saturday pm to play and watch sport `A02`. It also meant that wages were paid to workers, which gradually increased `A01`. This gave the working class more money to spend on sport (e.g. to pay for football ground admission) `A02`. Factory owners encouraged sporting involvement among their workers `A01` by setting up factory teams, for example Arsenal originated at a weapons-making factory `A02`.

3/8 marks awarded This is a basic attempt at providing breadth/depth of relevant points, and also fails to gain any credit for evaluation (A03), which further limits its mark.

Question 5

Identify and explain the social factors that led to the emergence of mass spectator sport in the nineteenth century.

[8 marks]

This question requires you to identify a range of different social factors covered in the specification and link them to how they contributed positively to large numbers of people going to watch sports such as football.

Student A answer

In the nineteenth century, working conditions improved in factories `A01`. For example, there was a decrease in working hours, as well as increased wages `A02`. This had the positive outcome of providing more money to pay for gate entrance fees to watch matches, as well as free time on Saturday afternoons to do it `A03`.

There were also improvements in transport in the nineteenth century `A01`. Developments in steam trains made it easier for the masses to attend football matches and reach different parts of the country `A02`. This meant that more fixtures were scheduled for the masses to watch on a home and away basis `A03`.

Another social factor leading to mass spectator sport was improved literacy, which aided the development of improved communications to the working class `A01`. For example, the development of newspapers enabled far more awareness of sport `A02`. This was very positive for spectatorism because it created far more interest in/awareness of sport via details of when/where fixtures were taking place `A03`.

Finally, a very important factor in the development of spectator sport was urbanisation `A01`. It was important because it led to large numbers of people moving en-mass into towns and cities, and the masses needed entertaining `A02`. Sport in the newly created purpose-built stadia in the limited urban space available was an ideal opportunity for large numbers to spectate `A03`.

7/8 marks awarded This level 4 answer expresses knowledge in a consistently accurate and detailed manner. Analysis and evaluative comments linked to the importance of the factors stated are also clearly evident. There is a clear structure and relevant focus to the answer throughout.

Student B answer

There were lots of social factors that helped sport develop in a rational way in nineteenth-century Britain. They included the development of steam trains A01, which meant you could travel into the countryside more to take part in activities like rambling. Factory owners helped sport develop by setting up works teams for their workers to play sports like football. They also improved working conditions A01 and gave more time off on Saturday afternoons to go and watch sports like rugby league and football A02. Urbanisation occurred, where large numbers moved into cities looking for work A01. This meant that there was less space available to play mob games, which meant new forms of sport had to emerge to participate in, like football.

2/8 marks awarded The limited knowledge evident in relation to the question set puts this in level 1. On occasions it links in an irrelevant way to positive impacts on performers as opposed to spectators. There is little, if any, analysis/evaluation evident in the answer, but it does have a reasonable structure to it.

Post World War 2 (1950 to present)

Question 6

Explain the benefits of sponsorship to companies investing large amounts of money in sport.   [3 marks]

This question requires you to focus on the positive outcomes for businesses arising from an involvement in sports sponsorship.

Student A answer

It increases sales and profits due to increased advertising of their products ✓. It also creates a positive association between a brand/product and the healthy image of sport ✓. Sporting events are often used for corporate hospitality (i.e. entertaining clients) to create more business opportunities ✓.

3/3 marks awarded This is an excellent answer, which makes three correct points with the necessary detail for an 'explain' question.

Student B answer

- Increases advertisement of products.
- Gives tax advantages.
- Creates more role models.

0/3 marks awarded The first two points are potentially creditworthy, but they lack the detail/use of link words required by the command word at the start of the question, i.e. 'explain'.

Question 7

Outline and evaluate the factors responsible for the advancement in opportunities for women to participate in sports such as football since the end of World War 2.

[6 marks]

> This question requires you to identify and explain a range of important factors that have positively influenced women's participation in football.

Student A answer

A number of sociocultural factors can be identified that have led to an increase in opportunities for women to participate and progress through to elite level in activities such as football in modern-day society.

First, there has been an increase in equal opportunities A01. More sports are generally available and socially acceptable for women to play, including football. Legally, the Sex Discrimination Act has been passed, leading to less sexual discrimination in sport A02. This has been of huge assistance in more women being able to play football at all levels of ability, including professionally A03.

Second, more recently there has been increased media coverage of women's football A01. BT Sport, for example, provides live coverage of the Women's Super League (WSL). This has generated more finance/sponsorship via partners such as Continental, Nike, SSE and Vauxhall A02. More female role models in women's football have also been created, further encouraging female participation in the sport A03.

Finally, in recent times there has been increased approval and encouragement of women's football from the FA A01. This contrasts with their earlier negative stance on the game in the twentieth century, when they effectively banned it A02. Now, however, they invest heavily in the game and have created central contracts for England players, which means a limited number can devote themselves full time to football A03.

6/6 marks awarded This excellent answer makes a number of knowledge/application and evaluation points relatively succinctly and in a well-structured, logical manner. It reads well and illustrates a very high level of understanding of the question set.

Student B answer

The roles played by women in support of the war effort were a factor in women being able to play football A01. Since World War 2 women have had an increase in leisure time available to participate in such sports as well as an increase in disposable income A01. They have also been helped by an increase in the number of clubs to join and the fact there are more role models A01.

2/6 marks awarded This answer is marked in the bottom band. It makes a number of knowledge points that require further explanation/development to gain credit for the other assessment objectives used to assess such extended-response questions.

The impact of sport on society and of society on sport

Question 8

Explain the benefits to society of increasing participation rates in sport and physical activity. [3 marks]

This question requires you to give relatively detailed answers linked to societal benefits (not individual benefits) of increased involvement in physical activity.

Student A answer

Increased physical activity improves a person's fitness levels, which can help decrease obesity and lessen the strain on the NHS ✓. It can also involve lots of people coming together to participate, which helps with community integration ✓. Finally, it can provide a positive use of free time, which helps keep people out of trouble and decreases the crime statistics ✓.

3/3 marks awarded This is an excellent answer, with three correct points explained well in relation to the question asked (i.e. the benefits of activity to society).

Student B answer

If you take part in more sport, it helps keep you occupied in your free time as well as improving your health and fitness. It also provides lots of social contact (e.g. when you join a club).

0/3 marks awarded These points are irrelevant because they relate to the benefits of increased activity to the individual, whereas the question set requires positive outcomes linked to society.

Question 9

Identify three barriers to sports participation that still exist for ethnic minority groups in twenty-first-century Britain. [3 marks]

This question requires you to give three correct answers, avoiding repetition of similar points because only the first three answers will be credited.

Student A answer

- There is sometimes conflict with religious observances such as dress codes ✓.
- Discrimination still occurs (e.g. racist chants to a player) ✓.
- Stereotyping/channelling still affects the sports participated in by ethnic minorities ✓.

3/3 marks awarded Three clear/correct points linked to the question set.

Student B answer

- Fewer role models to aspire to ✓.
- Less media coverage publicising ethnic minority sport.
- Less time to do sport.

1/3 marks awarded The first two answers are relatively similar, so as repeated points they can only be credited once. The final answer is too vague and needs to link to how ethnicity can negatively affect sports participation.

Question 10

Define, using examples, the following terms:

(a) Discrimination

(b) Stereotyping   [2 marks]

> Do not forget to include examples in your answer. Definitions alone will not be credited.

Student A answer

Discrimination is the unfair treatment of a person, often based on a stereotype, for example lack of access to a club for a wheelchair user ✓.

A stereotype is a preconceived idea about a group in society that can negatively impact on their involvement in sport, for example the belief that women should not play certain power-based sports due to their 'non-aggressive' nature ✓.

2/2 marks awarded Correct definitions are given for both terms, along with appropriate examples, as required by the question set.

Student B answer

Discrimination is when an individual is treated unfairly and stereotyping is a set of beliefs about a particular group in society.

0/2 marks awarded No marks are awarded because no examples are given when defining the terms.

Question 11

A government consultation document published post-London 2012 described the number of disabled people taking part in sport as 'disappointingly low'. This was backed up by Sport England 'Active People' data that measured the number of disabled people active at least once a week as follows:

2012/13: 18.2%

2013/14: 17.4%

2014/15: 17.2%

2015/16: 16.8%

Using the disability participation data above, explain the barriers faced by disabled athletes and the effectiveness of the strategies used to overcome these barriers.   [15 marks]

> This question requires you to correctly interpret and analyse the data relating to disability participation in physical activity and sport, and relate this to barriers/solutions/evaluation of solutions as appropriate.

Student A answer

When analysing disability sports participation, there are a number of common barriers that negatively affect them and a range of solutions to such problems, as explained below.

Funding can be an issue affecting disability sport participation. Lack of investment in disability sport and low income levels, and the fact that statistically they are more likely to be on benefits, may mean that disabled people cannot afford the costs of participation, which may include entrance fees and specialist equipment A01.

Solutions to this include increased investment in disability sport via organisations such as Sport England and the Activity Alliance, as well as local councils who can provide local facilities at a cheaper/subsidised cost to access A02. However, this is less likely for local councils at the moment because they are having to make funding cuts due to decreased budgets from the government. However, it is still an investment priority for Sport England and its national partner Activity Alliance A03.

Many disabled individuals have a lack of self-confidence, which negatively affects their participation in sport, for example due to fear of failure/negative comments about their capabilities. This is not helped by a lack of media coverage of disabled sport (which also impacts on sponsorship opportunities) and limited awareness of disabled role models A01.

Solutions to this include providing more support and opportunities to be successful to disabled individuals taking up a sport, via specialist coaches, as well as getting more media coverage of disabled sport on TV. Channel 4 had a successful Paralympics 'meet the superhumans' campaign linked to their coverage of Rio 2016 and their 'Yes I can!' catchphrase A02.

Although there have been some improvements in the media coverage of Paralympic sport, it is still way below that of able-bodied sport and is often not sustained beyond Paralympic coverage A03.

Participation is on the decline, as illustrated by the Sport England Active People survey statistics above (e.g. a 1.4% decrease in once a week participation over the 4 years when the survey was undertaken) A03. An important reason for this is spread of negative myths and stereotypes surrounding disability sports performers that can lead to overt verbal discrimination and poor treatment A01. Solutions to this include educating people (e.g. sports coaches) about the negative myths and stereotypes and challenging inappropriate attitudes towards disability sport A02. One particularly good example of an Activity Alliance scheme designed to challenge stereotypes is 'GOGA', which promotes participation of disabled and non-disabled individuals in sport alongside one another A03.

13/15 marks awarded This level 5 answer demonstrates accurate/well detailed knowledge. Analysis and evaluation points are given in an ongoing manner throughout the answer, with relevant terms consistently used. There is a clear structure and relevant focus to the answer.

Student B answer

Barriers to participation include negative myths and stereotypes A01. These can be overcome by educating people on these stereotypes and what disabled people are actually capable of. Another barrier is access to sports facilities A01. This can be overcome by installing ramps for wheelchair users to access facilities A02. A third barrier is that disabled people often have low levels of income and cannot afford participation/equipment costs A01. This barrier can be overcome by subsidising disabled sport and making it more affordable A02. Fourthly, they often suffer from a lack of confidence and believe sport is not for them A01. This can be overcome by letting them participate in sports in which they can be successful A02.

4/15 marks awarded This answer demonstrates some accurate knowledge of barriers, with linked applications evident via suggested solutions to help overcome them. There are no evaluation points evident or links to the data, with the answer simply outlining a few barriers/solutions, with very little evidence of substantiated reasoning.

Knowledge check answers

1 It lowers bad LDL cholesterol levels and significantly increases good HDL cholesterol levels.

2 It is higher; it benefits performance because more blood, and therefore more oxygen, is transported to the working muscles.

3 Training results in cardiac hypertrophy/an increase muscle mass. This means there is an increase in stroke volume and a reduction in resting heart rate/bradycardia.

The reduced heart rate allows for a longer diastolic phase. Consequently there is an increase in the ejection fraction. There is also a greater heart rate range and an increase in maximal cardiac output.

4 The SAN sends impulses through the walls of the atria, causing them to contract (atrial systole). The impulse then passes through the AVN and onto the bundle of His, which branches into two bundle branches and into the Purkinje fibres. These spread the impulse throughout the ventricles, causing them to contract (ventricular systole).

5 An increase in carbon dioxide is picked up by chemoreceptors. These send impulses to the cardiac control centre in the medulla oblongata. Sympathetic impulses are then sent to the SAN to increase heart rate.

6 Haemoglobin transports oxygen in the blood. Myoglobin stores oxygen in the muscles.

7 Tidal volume will be represented by lines that are closer together to show faster breathing and much taller to show deeper breathing. Residual volume will remain the same.

8 Definition of diffusion: high concentration/partial pressure to low concentration/partial pressure/down a concentration/diffusion gradient.
   - pO_2/concentration higher in blood and lower in muscle.
   - Moves/diffuses from blood/capillary to muscle.
   - pCO_2/concentration higher in muscle and lower in blood.
   - Moves/diffuses from muscle to blood/capillary.

9 Smoking reduces the oxygen-carrying capacity of the blood, which reduces the ability to work aerobically. Therefore, the performer fatigues more quickly because they have to work more anaerobically.

10 Type I

11 When there is stretch in the muscle.

12 When there is tension in the muscle.

13

Joint action	Hip abduction	Knee extension
Plane and axis	Frontal plane and sagittal axis	Sagittal plane and transverse axis
Agonist	Gluteus medius or gluteus minimus	Quadriceps
Antagonist	Adductors	Hamstrings

14 For high-intensity activities lasting less than 10 seconds, anaerobic respiration/no O_2. Creatine kinase is the enzyme that breaks down the PC that is stored in the muscles into creatine and phosphate. Energy is used/released for ATP synthesis; aerobic energy is needed for recovery.

15 Any three from:
   - intensity of exercise
   - slow-twitch fibres producing less lactate than fast-twitch fibres
   - VO_2 max of a performer/buffering
   - a respiratory exchange ratio close to 1.0
   - fitness of performer

16
   - ATP-PC system — any highly explosive activity lasting fewer than 10 seconds, such as a short sprint for the ball.
   - Anaerobic glycolytic system — a longer, high-intensity example, for example making a break in rugby to sprint the length of the pitch.
   - Aerobic — low intensity, high duration example, for example positional play.

17
   - Restoration of ATP and PC.
   - Resaturation of myoglobin with oxygen.

18 Skilful performers:
   - have learned their skills
   - are efficient/economical
   - are effortless
   - have a goal in mind
   - are consistent/accurate

19 Massed practice is continuous with no rest periods, whereas distributed practice allows rest periods for recovery, feedback and mental rehearsal.

20 Low organisation, serial, complex and/or dangerous skills.

21 Extrinsic, positive and some knowledge of results.

22 A sharp increase in success rate, increased fluency in movement, high motivation.

23 Attention, retention, motor reproduction, motivation.

24 What the learner can do when the MKO helps:
   - Stage 1 — what the performer can achieve independently.
   - Stage 2 — what the performer can achieve with help from the MKO.
   - Stage 3 — what the performer cannot do at this moment in time.

25
   - Effective for cognitive performers.
   - Useful in dangerous tasks as it improves safety during performance.
   - Reduces fear/anxiety.
   - Builds confidence.
   - Whole skill can be attempted.
   - Develops kinaesthesis.

26 Knowledge of results tells you if the skill was successful or not. Knowledge of performance gives you technical information about why the action was successful or unsuccessful.

27 Senses gather cues from the display:
- Eyes — vision
- Ears — audition
- Proprioceptors — touch, balance and kinaesthesis

Selective attention is operational.

28 It holds visual and spatial information temporarily. It also stores kinaesthetic information about how the movement feels.

29 It sends impulses to the working muscles to carry out the movement.

30 Temporal anticipation — predicting when the stimulus will be presented. Spatial anticipation — predicting where and what is going to happen.

31 An additional stimulus has arrived before the first has been processed.

32 Information is gathered about the movement using intrinsic feedback or kinaesthesis — how the movement feels/looks.

33 Local, basic, low-level rule structure, violent, occasional, rural, natural, clear class divisions evident.

34
- Played by upper-class males as an exclusively upper-class activity.
- Played with complex rules because the upper class were educated and therefore highly literate.
- Played to a high moral code, which reflected the civilised lifestyle of the upper class.
- Played regularly in a highly skilled manner because the upper class were the 'leisured class'.
- Played in purpose-built facilities with specialist equipment because the upper class were wealthy.
- Non-local in nature because the upper class had the ability to travel.

35
- Lack of space (space was at a premium) — led to the development of purpose-built facilities to play sport (e.g. football grounds).
- Large working-class populations — needed entertaining, resulting in mass spectator numbers at football matches for the first time.
- Loss of traditional sports — many traditional working-class sports, such as mob games, were banned in a civilised society, so there was a need for new sports to emerge.

36
- The approval/active involvement of the clergy gave encouragement for the working classes to participate in rationalised sporting activities (e.g. association football).
- The Church organised/set up clubs.
- The Church provided facilities to play sport (e.g. church halls/playing fields).
- A number of church groups formed, with sporting involvement a key part of their programmes of activities (e.g. the YMCA).

37
- Highly structured/codified, with set rules (e.g. pitch dimensions).
- Institutionalised/had a national governing body (e.g. the FA).
- Had officials (e.g. referees).
- Played for extrinsic rewards (e.g. high wages/medals).
- Highly skilled/involved strategies and tactics (e.g. use of set plays to score).

38 Due to negative myths/restrictions, such as:
- traditional viewpoint that sport was a 'male preserve'
- sport evolved from aggressive/violent activities (e.g. mob games)
- sport viewed as 'too aggressive'/'too competitive' for women and led to 'over exertion'
- belief in early twentieth century that sports participation had a negative impact on fertility/child-bearing capacity
- women being restricted by the clothing they had to wear (corsets/long dresses)

39 Interest in high-profile sports; visually appealing; high skill levels; well-matched competition; simple rules.

40 (a) Primary socialisation is socialisation during the early years of childhood via the immediate family, for example parents/siblings.

(b) Secondary socialisation is socialisation that occurs during the 'later years', i.e. as teenagers/adults via agencies such as schools, the media and friends.

41
- Social stratification involves social inequality, where society is divided into different levels based on social class (e.g. based on wealth).
- Disposable income/wealth can impact on participation in a positive or negative way.
- High-income earners can afford a wider variety of sports (e.g. expensive ones such as equestrianism), in contrast to low-income earners, who have more limited/restricted opportunities.
- High-income earners are able to afford a healthy diet, which helps health and fitness levels as part of an overall healthy lifestyle. Low-income earners tend to purchase cheaper, less healthy options.
- Social stratification can affect which sports are traditionally participated in, for example the middle class are associated with hockey and tennis; the working class with boxing and rugby league.

42 D

43
- Improved communication/teamwork/cooperative skills.
- Increased ability to make friends with people of shared interests.
- More positive outlook on life, so become more approachable/increased confidence to interact with others/be in the company of others.

Index

Index